D1474298

Teaching Exceptional Children
Assessing and Modifying Social Behavior

EDUCATIONAL PSYCHOLOGY

Allen J. Edwards, Series Editor
Department of Psychology
Southwest Missouri State University
Springfield, Missouri

Phillip S. Strain, Thomas P. Cooke, and Tony Apolloni. Teaching Exceptional Children: Assessing and Modifying Social Behavior

In preparation:

Donald E. P. Smith and others. A Technology of Reading and Writing (in four volumes). Vol. 1. Learning to Read and Write: A Task Analysis (By Donald E. P. Smith).

Gilbert R. Austin. Early Childhood Education: An International Perspective

Vernon L. Allen and Joel R. Levin (eds.). Cognitive Learning in Children: Theories and Strategies

Vernon L. Allen (ed.). Children as Teachers: Theory and Research on Tutoring

António Simões (ed.). The Bilingual Child: Research and Analysis of Existing Educational Themes

Teaching Exceptional Children
Assessing and Modifying Social Behavior

Phillip S. Strain
School of Education
American University
Washington, D. C.

Thomas P. Cooke
Tony Apolloni
Department of Special Education
California State College at Sonoma
Rohnert Park, California

ACADEMIC PRESS New York San Francisco London 1976

A Subsidiary of Harcourt Brace Jovanovich, Publishers

To our friend and teacher, Richard E. Shores,
who prompted and reinforced our initial
attempts at scientific inquiry

ACADEMIC PRESS, INC.
111 Fifth Avenue, New York, New York 10003

371.9
S896t
1976

United Kingdom Edition published by
ACADEMIC PRESS, INC. (LONDON) LTD.
24/28 Oval Road, London NW1

Library of Congress Cataloging in Publication Data

Strain, Phillip S
    Teaching exceptional children.

    (Educational psychology monographs)
    Includes bibliographies and index.
    1.   Exceptional children–Education.   2.   Sociali-
zation.   3.   Behavior modification.   I.   Cooke,
Thomas P., joint author.   II.   Apolloni, Tony, joint
author.   III.   Title.   [DNLM: 1.   Behavior therapy–
In infancy and childhood.   2.   Social behavior–In
infancy and childhood.   3.   Child, Exceptional.
4.   Child development deviations.   WM420 S897a]
LC3969.S87   371.9   75-19679
ISBN 0–12–673450–X

Contents

Preface

Throughout the history of the American educational enterprise, only sporadic attention has been given to the social–emotional development of children (Beatty, 1969; Sandiford, 1936; Thorndike, 1906). With the current expansion of educational services for exceptional children, many special as well as "regular" educators have become aware of the need for instructional strategies to ameliorate delayed or deviant social–emotional behavior of students.

Those educators who have addressed the issue of social–emotional education have contributed significantly to exposing our lack of empirical evidence regarding the development and modification of social interaction patterns. Regrettably, these indictments (for example, see Henderson, 1972; Lyon, 1971) have generated, to date, little naturalistic research that attempts to describe the parameters of social–emotional development, and even fewer manipulative studies that evaluate the effectiveness of educational interventions designed to increase prosocial behavior.

It is our collective bias (although we maintain that our bias rests on empirical data) that the basic operating principles of human behavior generated by the experimental analysis of behavior (Skinner, 1953) provide both a sound conceptualization of social–emotional behavior and a wealth of empirically validated treatment techniques which may be used to accelerate children's prosocial behavior.

This volume is divided into three somewhat overlapping chapters. In Chapter 1, we trace the history of social–emotional education, review various theories of social–emotional development, provide a limited review of research on selected parameters of social–emotional development, and suggest the potential contribution of operant learning principles to social–emotional education. In Chapter 2, we discuss the relationship between theories of social–emotional development and the unit of measurement, or dependent variables, selected for study in social–emotional research. Specifically, social drive–social reinforcement, dyadic or response support, and ethological theories are reviewed. Observational and experimental methodologies associated with each position are critically reviewed in terms of the reliability and validity of the unit of measurement employed. Finally, a consolidation of methodologies is suggested in order to assess the enormous complexities of social behavior. In the final chapter, educational interventions designed to increase prosocial behavior are reviewed. Particular attention is given to the issue of behavior generalization across time and settings.

References

Beatty, W. H. Emotions: The missing link in education. *Theory into Practice,* 1969, *8,* 86–92.

Henderson, L. A. A review of the literature on affective education. *Contemporary Education,* 1972, *44,* 92–99.

Lyon, H. C. *Learning to feel—feeling to learn.* Columbus, Ohio: Charles E. Merrill, 1971.

Sandiford, P. *Educational psychology: An objective study.* New York: Longmans, Green, 1936.

Skinner, B. F. *Science and human behavior.* New York: Free Press, 1953.

Thorndike, E. *The principles of teaching.* New York: A. G. Seller, 1906.

Introduction

The belief that the American educational institution has been negligent in its attention to systematic methods and strategies for enhancing the social–emotional dimension of child development is now widely held. This notion is not merely the position of an esoteric group of professionals, but has been noted by commentators across the fields of education (Borich, 1971; Harbeck, 1970; Morris, 1972), special education (Bradtke, Kirkpatrick, & Rosenblatt, 1972; Morse, 1971), humanistic psychology (Henderson, 1972; Lyon, 1971; Rogers, 1969, 1970), and behavioral psychology (Homme, 1970; Ivey, 1969; Lazarus, 1973; Winnett & Winkler, 1972).

The significance of effective educational intervention in the emotional realm of children has been noted even by the progenitors of current pedagogy. Thorndike (1906) has observed that not only is the guidance of social and emotional development properly a major concern of education but educators must mold an emotional commitment in students to maximize cognitive and intellectual growth. Sandiford (1936) has made perhaps a more direct contribution to modern educational thought in this area by writing, "the influence of emotion is so strong that one can hardly understand human behavior without understanding the accompanying affective states. Certainly, one cannot hope to promote learning without utilizing the powerful motivational push of the emotions" (pp. 130–131). Although Thorndike and Sandiford wrote their respective treatises a full 30 years apart, they were in agreement that the educational institution ought justifiably place more emphasis on the social–emotional guidance of children.

Prescott (1938) has compiled an early literature review on the role of emotion in the educational process—specifically, on the education of the emotions. He has concluded from his review of theoretical and empirical literature that emotions play a significant role in inhibiting or enhancing learning. Prescott (1938) has noted, nearly 40 years ago, the value of directing the scientific and applied resources of education to the training of the emotions. Since the time of his writing, however, little more systematic analysis of emotional education has been conducted.

Beatty (1969) has reacted to this deficiency by referring to the emotions as "the missing link in education" (p. 86). Beatty has maintained that, for schools to foster the development of desirable emotional behavior, teachers must instruct their pupils in a fashion much different from that currently employed. Other commentators not only have expressed dissatisfaction with the lack of emphasis on social–emotional training but have posited serious consequences resulting from this deficit. Lyon (1971) has argued that the educational institution is responsible for developing what he terms "intellectual half men" (p. 21) as a result of placing total emphasis on academic and intellectual development of children to the exclusion of social–emotional considerations. Lyon has maintained that, as long as this state of priorities exists, school children will realize only half of their full human potential. Weinstein and Fantini (1970) have presented the position that education of children's emotions offers more behavior-change potency than purely academic learning. These authors have stressed the importance of teaching humanitarianism to children and have maintained that the training of positive emotional behaviors in children is the only way to achieve this goal. Borich (1971) has advanced the position that social–emotional development seems to have more impact than cognitive development on determining success or failure, adaptation or maladaptation in school, as well as in society at large. If Borich's position is valid, it seems that the popular academic orientation of schools is counterproductive in terms of their ultimate goal of preparing citizens to function in a myriad of social environments.

Morse (1971) has noted the importance of an emotional-behavior training component in programs of special education. He has maintained that children with problems requiring special educational services should receive even more systematic attention to social–emotional development than "normal" children. He has forwarded the belief that ineptness in emotional behavior is one of the key areas of difficulty of children termed "exceptional." Moreover, Morse has held that it is because teachers do not understand the processes involved in emotional training that they are prone to use haphazard techniques that are ineffective in teaching desirable emotional-behavior patterns. He has noted that although the education of the emotions is often lauded as needed and worthwhile, it is usually discussed in terms of "vaguely worded advice" (p. 67) that is impossible to translate into educational methodology. As an alternative, Morse has suggested the development of specific-skill training for teachers in emotionally oriented education.

Schrag (1972) has maintained that mental illness in children often may be the result of absent or inadequate training in how to control emotional behavior. Schrag has advanced the position that, if the same kind of emotional nurturance characteristic of psychotherapy were incorporated into educational practice, the incidence of emotional and mental health problems of children would decrease dramatically. If Schrag is correct, even partially, in his assertions, the implications for the field of special education are of great significance.

Many other investigators, perhaps thinking along more pragmatic lines, have noted that, even though social–emotional education is indeed a critical and largely overlooked area, little is to be gained by glittering statements of its importance or ominous threats regarding its continued omission. Rather, it has been held that accountable techniques capable of withstanding empirical tests of effectiveness are needed to demonstrate conclusively the value of emotional education. Borich (1971), for example, has agreed with the previously cited authors that the educational institution is seriously remiss in continuing to ignore the education of the emotions. He has elaborated this position, however, by advocating that schools should not attend to the emotional dimension of education, but must develop accountable techniques in this area. Borich has concluded that, without accountability in emotional education, schools may continue to shun their responsibility for this critical area of their charges' development.

Harbeck (1970) has concurred with Borich (1971) through her suggestion that educators can no longer justify inferential assumptions or a reliance on haphazard contingencies in the training of the emotions. She has maintained that school personnel must begin to measure objectively the subjective feelings on which they have relied in the past. Harbeck has conceded the difficulty of the task, but has underscored the notion that difficulty is no excuse for continued neglect. "It seems safer to conscientiously work on evaluation in this area than to leave it to chance and to hope for the best" (Harbeck, 1970, p. 52). Hirschlein and Jones (1971) have made essentially the same demand for objectifying emotional education in spite of the inherent difficulties of the task. They have added that "the development of more systematic methods for achieving emotional education objectives is an integral part of curriculum planning" (p. 47).

Thus, it seems apparent that minimal attention has been directed to emotional education. This is not to say, however, that no work in this area has been undertaken. In fact, several well-known educators and psychologists have attempted to develop models and curricula for emotional education. However, upon critical review, it becomes evident that the bulk of this work is unaccountable for its efforts, thereby becoming subject to Borich's (1971) criticism of actually shunning responsibility. Additionally, current efforts in emotional education seem to rely on the "vaguely worded advice" (p. 67) condemned by Morse (1971) and the "haphazard contingencies" (p. 49) noted as characteristic by Harbeck (1970).

Weinstein and Fantini (1970) have written one of the most renowned books in emotional education: *Toward humanistic education: A curriculum of affect*. Although this book has purported to offer an entire model curriculum for emotional education, the authors have acknowledged that there exists no empirical evidence to substantiate its worth. Additionally, although the authors have supported "a change in behavior" (p. 43) as being the definition of learning, their curriculum lacks any objective techniques for monitoring such change.

Ellis (1971) has developed a methodology for reducing the emotional-behavior problems of children. His technique, termed "rational–emotive therapy," approaches emotional problems with a series of games and activities designed to educate children to their own emotionality. Ellis has claimed that his technique can be used by teachers and has classroom applicability. Unfortunately, Ellis has conceded that his methods are not yet sufficiently refined to bear up under the scrutiny of empirical investigation. Thus, another attempt at emotional education is limited in general applicability owing to a lack of accountability.

Other emotional educators, such as Gregg (1971) and Rogers (1970), have used paper and pencil instruments to gauge the effect of treatment in the emotional realm. Unfortunately, however, the general lack of validity of such instruments for detecting and measuring real-life behavioral change prohibits their acceptance by many scientists (McClelland, 1973; Popham, 1971; Skinner, 1953).

Henderson (1972) recently has reviewed the literature in emotional education. Although he has lauded many of the pioneers in the area, such as Jonathan Kozol, George Lenard, and Johnathan Kohl, Henderson has simultaneously acknowledged that these emotional educators have not operated from an empirical base of support. It seems clear that such attempts have been prone to maintain emotional education as an art, rather than to advance it as a science or as a series of methods that may be taught to teachers in professional training. If emotional education is to become widespread, effective teacher training is an obvious necessity.

Lyon (1971), after a comprehensive review of attempts to empirically validate emotional education, has concluded that substantial evidence of its worth is sadly lacking. He has inferred that the explanation for this deficiency of evaluative data is that those involved in emotional education have become so invested in the joy it produces that they have been unwilling to back away and objectively investigate the phenomena. Lyon has added, however, that nothing less than rigorous data-based evaluation, substantiating the value of emotional education, will suffice to produce significant impact on the American educational institution.

As Lyon has suggested, in order for emotional training to become operationalized and widespread, the techniques must possess replicability and must successfully endure empirical tests of their effectiveness. Many of the approaches discussed thus far have represented admirable attempts to treat emotional behavior. In fact, it seems plausible that some of the techniques may produce the dramatic effects so often anecdotally reported by their developers and participants. The fact that so many methods of emotional education are unsupported by data does not mean that they are failures. However, their uniform lack of an empirical base has prevented definitive conclusions concerning their effectiveness from being drawn. Moreover, their lack of replicability gives rise to serious questions of their validity, since replicability has been considered the essence of believability by applied-behavioral scientists (Baer, Wolf, & Risley, 1968).

It appears as though the field of social–emotional education is currently victimized by a paradox. On the one side there is widespread agreement that social–emotional education is an important area that has been too long neglected. Much of this neglect has been based on the skepticism of educational decision makers concerning the value and accountability of intervention in the emotional realm of children. The other side of the paradox has been that the educators and psychologists who have responded to the need for methodology and curricula of emotional education have done so from a mentalistic perspective, largely without reliance on the principles of accountability, replicability, and empirical validation. Such attempts, however well-intentioned, may inadvertently maintain and reinforce the previously mentioned skepticism and thus function counterproductively. It appears that one approach to solving this dilemma involves the application of behavioral principles (Baer *et al.*, 1968) and methodology (Bijou, Peterson, Harris, Allen, & Johnson, 1969) to the field of emotional education.

Behavioristic investigators have avoided mentalistic constructs in emotion and have considered emotional-behavior change as the "raison d'etre" of emotional treatment or education. Skinner (1953) has pointed out that the only way of determining the presence or absence of emotion is through systematically monitoring emotional behavior. Moreover, he has suggested that a practical technology of emotional treatment depends on a behavioral orientation to the area.

> As long as we conceive of the problem of emotion as one of inner states, we are not likely to advance a practical technology. It does not help in the solution of a practical problem to be told that some feature of a man's behavior is due to frustration or anxiety; we also need to be told how the frustration or anxiety has been induced and how it may be altered. In the end, we find ourselves dealing with two events—the emotional behavior and the manipulable conditions of which the behavior is a function. [Skinner, 1953, p. 167]

Although theoreticians and scientists will, no doubt, long continue to debate this issue, its implications of utility and efficacy for emotional educators seem apparent. Although hypothesized internal or mentalistic constructs have often been associated with emotion (Arnold, 1970), these phenomena are too abstract and theoretical to be measured and treated by teachers. In any event, it

has been pointed out (Day, 1969) that insofar as a phenomonologi-
cally oriented individual is in contact with human functioning, he
can only observe and respond to behavior. Another group of
scientists (Blatz, 1923; Thompson, 1967) have held that emotion is
best measured in a laboratory setting, utilizing such indices as
galvanic skin response and heart rate. Such measurements of
emotion, however, are obviously unavailable to educational practitioners. It can be derived, then, that given current technology in
the measurement of emotion, observable behavior is the most
functional index for use by emotional educators. Thus, behavioral
teaching strategies could be valuable tools in emotional education.
Additionally, a behavior-analytic approach seems justified since
behavioral techniques of intervention have been successfully utilized by teachers in natural classroom environments to achieve a
wide variety of educational goals (see O'Leary & O'Leary, 1972).

While behavior-analytic scientists and practitioners have made
great contributions to the fields of education and special education
(see O'Leary & O'Leary, 1972; Ulrich, Stachnik, & Mabry, 1970;
Wallace & Kauffman, 1973), they have not contributed significantly
to the area of emotional education. This perhaps results from the
fact that operational definitions of behaviors have been required
by behaviorists as prerequisites for any investigation. Such definitions are critical since behavioral scientists are committed to
studying events that are observable, countable, and repeatable
(Cartwright & Cartwright, 1974; Wallace & Kauffman, 1973). Emotional educators, on the other hand, traditionally have used such
subjective terms as "friendliness," "humanitarianism," and "helpfulness" to describe the goals of their endeavors.

If operational definitions of emotional-education goals were
developed, the behavioral paradigm could contribute greatly to the
field of emotional education. Although this has not been done
previously, it seems entirely possible since there exist no "rules"
either implicit or implied, that preclude the operationalizing and
behavioral investigation of any area of human behavior (Sidman,
1960; Skinner, 1974).

Viewed from a behavioral perspective, then, a prerequisite for
research and development in emotional education is the determination of what is actually meant by emotional educators when they
indicate that a child should be friendly, humanitarian, or helpful.
Such behaviors as smiling, verbally complimenting, positively phys-

ically contacting, and sharing would seem to be behavioral manifestations of the previously mentioned emotional states of children. Given current technology, these behavioral manifestations of
emotion are highly functional measures of the success of emotional education.

Such a liaison between emotional education and behavioral
psychology could add a new dimension to behavioristic research.
The current status of behavioral psychology is delimited by an
overriding concern with reducing negative emotional behaviors
and a relatively uncomprehensive consideration of training positive
or desirable emotional behaviors (see O'Leary & O'Leary, 1972).
Bandura (1969) has pointed out that behavioristic scientists have
largely overlooked the enormously important area of using positive
reinforcements to develop systematically such emotional behaviors
as empathy, friendliness, pleasurable reactions, and favorable
social attitudes. This deficiency in operant research has been
reiterated by Reynolds (1968), who has held that, even though such
negative emotions as fear and anxiety have been studied in depth,
the "tender emotions" have been largely neglected by operant
scientists.

Although not writing from a behavioristic perspective, Peters
(1970), in his work on the education of the emotions, has made a
point that reinforces that of Bandura (1969) and Reynolds (1968).
Peters has maintained that one of the primary tasks in the education of the emotions is fostering in children a capacity for objectivity. He has suggested converting the natural curiosity of children
into a desire for truth as a goal of emotional education. The
condition Peters has despaired is that, while psychology has told us
much about the conditions under which irrationality or negative
affect develops, it has told us little of the conditions which foster
rationality or positive affect in children.

As outlined earlier, heavy emphasis and great resources have
been applied to reducing negative emotional behavior, such as
fear, anger, and aggression, whereas little attention has been paid
to the development of positive affective behaviors, such as kind-
ness, fairness, and love. Winnett and Winkler (1972) have arrived at
much the same conclusion. They have accused behavior modifiers
of consistent attention to the negative side of behavior control and
lack of attention to using operant technology to engineer for
humanitarian virtues. They have written that the bulk of the

behavior modification literature has reported attempts to make children "still, docile, and quiet" (Winnett & Winkler, 1972, p. 499). They have accused behavior modifiers of seeking a repressive, antihuman control. However, these writers have not been without alternative suggestions. They have pointed out that they believe in the worth of behavior modification and are convinced of its potential in helping bring about positive change in schools and in society. However, they have emphasized using the technology to engineer for freedom and happiness rather than for repression and docility.

Thus, it can be seen that an application of behavioral psychology to emotional education would answer such critics as Bandura (1969), Reynolds (1968), and Peters (1970) by directing investigation toward the development of positive emotional behaviors in children. Additionally, such an effort would respond to Winnett and Winkler (1972), who have accused behaviorists of repressing the behaviors of children. This behavioral research of emotional education should focus on the acceleration of positive emotional behavior rather than the deceleration of emotional behavior considered inappropriate.

The contribution of behavioral research to emotional education could be of great significance. It was pointed out previously that affective educators have been unable to demonstrate empirically the value of their discipline. Moreover, they have been unable to demonstrate replicability or accountability. This failure has been held responsible for the often-noted narrow acceptance and limited impact of affective education. If objective and reliable behavioral data were added to affective education as an accountability device, the field would gain the power of empirical support. Additionally, such an empirically based emotional-education thrust would add replicability, generalizability, and accountability to the field. It has been pointed out frequently (Borich, 1971; Lyon, 1971; Morris, 1972; Morse, 1971) that, when emotional education gains these qualities, it will increase greatly in scope and impact.

Theories of Social–Emotional Development

There exists currently a variety of theoretical positions regarding the social–emotional or affective development of children. Many theorists have advanced hypotheses that they feel reveal reasonable outlines of normative social–emotional development. However, not all such theorists have approached the study of this development from the same perspective. In fact, it often appears that the variety of theories in existence is sufficiently divergent to cause theoretical conflicts or paradigm clashes in the field. Nevertheless, every major theoretical school of social–emotional development has supporters and advocates who believe adamantly in their respective positions. It seems accurate to maintain, in fact, that at least three broadly defined theoretical positions—the cognitive, the psychodynamic–maturational, and the behavioral—have had effects so pervasive on the development of our educational system that they may be viewed as "conventions" in education and psychology. For this reason, those interested in the establishment of a subdiscipline of education dedicated to the development of accountable and operational techniques in social–emotional training must attend to these theoretical positions in order to receive the acceptance of the educational community at large. Attention to these theories, however, must not supersede attention to the more significant requirement of accountability. The theories should be analyzed differentially, therefore, to glean theoretical support which is congruent with empirical research and accountability.

A comprehensive review of these theories would require voluminous tomes and is clearly beyond the scope of this work. Such reviews have been compiled and are available to the reader desiring in-depth theoretical study (Arnold, 1970; Bijou & Baer, 1961, 1965; Freud, 1954; Piaget, 1948). For the purposes of the present review, a brief overview of the three major theoretical positions mentioned earlier will suffice to demonstrate that these theories are a necessary foundation for work in social–emotional or affective education.

Piaget, Dewey, Montessori, and Bruner generally have been considered cognitive–developmental theorists (Ripple & Rockcastle, 1964). Owing to the recent focus on the educational significance of Piaget's theories (Kohlberg & Mayer, 1972), he seems an appropriate representative for discussion purposes.

Piaget has considered cognitive and emotional, or social (he uses the terms synonymously), development as parallel aspects of a child's total development (Athey & Rubadeau, 1970; Piaget & Inhelder, 1969). Moreover, he has posited that, in understanding the affective development of children, it is essential not to separate this area from the general structuration of behavior (Piaget & Inhelder, 1969). Piaget has not conceived of emotional development as a function of fixed genetic factors, direct biological maturation, or direct learning; rather, he has viewed it as a result of organism–environmental interactions (Athey & Rabadeau, 1970). He has stressed the importance of continuity and experience in social or affective development and the dependence of each future stage of development upon the successful implementation of past stages. He has drawn a distinction between development—spontaneous processes tied to the phenomenon of embryogenesis—and learning—that which is provoked by situations. Thus it can be seen that Piaget has considered social or affective development to be inseparably wedded to the total development of children. This theoretical construct has implications for social–emotional education. Since Piaget's widely accepted and scholarly writings have oriented the educational community to the importance of directing their efforts to the appropriate developmental stages of children, those involved in emotionally oriented education would do well to follow suit. This would suggest that affective educational procedures should be structured around the appropriate social–emotional or affective–developmental levels of children. This notion is sound in theory and follows a widely held propriety of education. Before the implications of the theory can be operationalized and implemented, however, empirical questions concerning the development of emotion in children must be considered. Much of this research will be discussed in a later section of this review.

Many have considered Erickson, Gesell, Adler, and the Freuds (Sigmund & Anna) to be psychodynamic–maturational theorists (Coles, 1970; Kohlberg & Mayer, 1972; Maier, 1965; Munroe, 1955). This school of theorists long considered stages of social–emotional development to be "embryological"; that is, a stage of development is thought to represent the total state of an organism at any given time (Kohlberg & Mayer, 1972). Stage descriptions, then, have been essential components of the maturational or psychodynamic theories of development. For example, Gesell has provided stage descriptions of normative behavior for various age periods (Gesell & Amatruda, 1945). Freud, of course, has postulated the now renowned "psychosexual" stages of development (Brill, 1938; Kohlberg & Mayer, 1972). It is postulated that mental illness may result from emotionally unhealthy experiences in the various stages of development (Brill, 1938). Generally, the psychodynamic–maturational theorists have assumed that social–emotional or affective development unfolds through heredity or prepatterned stages (Kohlberg & Mayer, 1972).

Jones (1960) has described education as "ideally inspiring or allowing free play to the natural, health-seeking symbolic process of ego synthesis" (p. 15). Like many within the psychoanalytic school of thought, Jones has held that social and intellectual development will be seriously inhibited unless emotional maturity is established as an unwavering goal of education.

Erickson's (1959) writing on the association modalities of childhood has suggested that a child's play and his general approach to his body, space, and time reveal his inner-developmental preoccupation. Since the psychodynamic–maturational theorists have held that healthy integration of a stage of development is contingent on psychologically healthy experience, and that play is the major function of a child's ego, it would follow that educators wishing to translate this theory into practice would consider play therapy and play analysis viable additions to the affective realm of schooling experience. Advocates of play therapy (Axline, 1947) have maintained that nondirected play operates within a child's natural medium of self-expression, offering growth experiences through opportunities to play out frustration, tension, insecurity, fear, and confusion. This school of thought has indicated that, by playing out such feelings, a child brings them to the surface, faces them, learns to control them, or abandons them in a "quality ego experience" (Axline, 1947; Maier, 1965). It has been suggested that teachers do not intervene during these sessions—no praise, no criticism, no comments—so that maximum therapeutic potential may be achieved (Axline, 1947; Maier, 1965).

It seems apparent from reviews of the literature in social–emotional or affective education (Henderson, 1972; Lyon, 1971) that the bulk of past and current practices in the area have relied on the psychodynamic (considered broadly) school of thought for their theoretical base of support. Unfortunately, however, attempts to translate psychodynamic theory into educational tactics have resulted in procedures and programs that rely on "vaguely worded advice" (Morse, 1971, p. 67) and "haphazard contingencies" (Harbeck, 1970, p. 49). Further, since even the developers and practitioners of such methods concede that their techniques cannot be subjected to empirical tests or bear up under accountability checks (Ellis, 1971; Weinstein Fantini, 1970), they may be seen as actually shunning their real responsibility to emotional education (Borich, 1971).

When discussing the behavioral theory of social–emotional development, the names of Watson, Skinner, Bandura, Bijou, and Baer often are considered (Kohlberg & Mayer, 1972; Maier, 1965). In this "environmental contingency" theory of development, the environment is seen as the source of energy directly or indirectly transmitted to, and accumulated in, a developing child (Bijou & Baer, 1961, 1965; Kohlberg & Mayer, 1972). The child in turn emits observable behavior, which is the primary data source for behaviorists. According to this school of thought, then, social–emotional development is dependent upon available environmental opportunities. Sears (Sears, Maccoby, & Levin, 1957) has placed special importance on the influence of parents and teachers on children's social development. He has stated that, since behavior essentially represents reinforced actions, development may be accurately viewed as a training process. A child's social–emotional behavior and development, consequently, is a function of how he is reared (Maier, 1965). Since behaviorists have maintained that environmental conditions determine development, they are largely unconcerned with attempting to delineate "developmental stages" that would be expected to occur solely as a function of maturation. Clearly, then, the behavioral perspective of social–emotional or affective development would focus on observable manifestations of emotional behavior rather than on intrapsychic or developmental states.

The behavioral theory of child development is yet untapped by social–emotional educators (Lyon, 1971). This neglect seems to be based on the assumption that behavioral theory will suffice to explain and analyze only the simplest of human behavior. The conclusion drawn by affective educators is that human emotion is far too complex and intertwined to be considered adequately by behavioral theory (Rogers, 1969). Although this controversy seems to rage as a perennial verbal battle in education and psychology (Rogers & Skinner, 1956), it is properly a research question.

It seems unfortunate that affective educators have largely overlooked the behavioral theory of development in seeking a foundation for their discipline, since the behavioral theorists have contributed more directly to educational practice than either the cognitive or the psychodynamic theorists. Many behavioral techniques, such as precision teaching (Meacham & Weisen, 1969), contingency contracting (Homme, Csanyi, Gonzales, & Rechs, 1969), and token economies (Kazdin & Bootzin, 1972), have made significant impact on recent educational intervention. No doubt much of this impact is attributable to the fact that behavioral strategies are accountable as a result of their emphasis on data-based information. That is, the success or failure of behavioral interventions is objectively observable and the procedures may be replicated. These seem to be precisely the attributes needed for affective education to become operationalized, gain the acceptance of the educational community, and receive broad implementation.

It has been noted that affective educators must be sensitive to the traditions of the academic community in order to maximize the chances of the advancement of their discipline (Lyon, 1971). The major theoretical positions on social–emotional development are an important backdrop for any interaction in the affective domain. A more important priority, however, seems to be attention to empirical data. Although school systems should not be confused with scientific laboratories in their reliance on a data base, they are dependent on reasonably systematic methods of information collection and usage. "Accountability" has become a catchword in all areas of education. With the passing of the "teacher as artist" notion, the concepts of objectivity, reliability, and replicability have become salient in new areas of education. It seems safe to maintain that any future attempt to spur change or innovation in educational practice will have to be supported by an empirical base. The task of affective educators, then, is to review past research and conduct new research that will serve to demonstrate the value and accountability of intervention in the emotional realm of children.

Early Research on Social–Emotional Development

Watson and his proteges and contemporaries are credited with the first experimental demonstrations of the learned nature of emotional behavior (Marx & Hillix, 1963). Watson's initial research interest in this area was to determine which emotions were learned and which were innate (Watson & Morgan, 1917). His strategy for investigating this question was to present stimuli to children which were known to produce emotional reactions in adults. Watson's measurement system consisted merely of narrative records of his observations. Watson reported his results in the following manner:

> After observing a large number of infants, especially during the first months of life, we suggest the following group of emotional reactions as belonging to the original and fundamental nature of man: fear, rage, and love (using love in approximately the same space that Freud used sex). [Watson & Morgan, 1917, p. 165]

True to the scientific method, Watson added that he did not claim that this list of three was exhaustive but, rather, that his observations of young infants did not reveal any greater number or diversity of emotional behaviors. In an effort to bring under laboratory control the emotional behaviors he had identified, Watson operationally defined the behaviors and identified several stimuli or setting events that elicited them (Watson & Morgan, 1917). Fear was defined as a sudden catching of breath, clutching randomly with the hands, puckering of the lips, and crying. Loud sounds and the removal of support were the two principle situations found to elicit fear in infants. Watson defined rage as screaming, stiffening of the body, slashing or striking movements of the hands and arms, kicking of the legs and feet, and holding the breath to the point of becoming flushed. Watson reported that hampering an infant's movements was the principle event that resulted in rage. The love response was defined by Watson as slightly more variable than fear or rage. If the infant had been crying, he ceased. He would begin to smile and attempt to gurgle or coo. In slightly older children (the exact age is unspecified), love behaviors were characterized by extending the arms in an attempt to grasp or cling to another person. Watson reported that the situations evoking love behaviors were patting, hugging, gentle rocking and stroking, or manipulating some erogenous zone.

Although Watson's paper enumerating three "innate" emotional behaviors of humans is cited widely, it lacked quantitative data. It included, rather, the subjective reporting of the observations of Watson and his colleagues. Perhaps the real value of the paper was that it stimulated a wealth of additional research and writing in the area of human emotional behavior.

It should be noted that Watson's early theory of three innate emotions was later refuted. Several subsequent investigations failed to substantiate Watson's conclusions in this regard (Marx & Hillix, 1963; Valentine & Wickens, 1949). Sherman (1927), for example, following an experimental paradigm similar to Watson's, demonstrated that observers judged a child's emotional reaction from the expected effect of the stimulus rather than from overt responses. Sherman's procedure was simply to show observers films of infants receiving some stimuli and reacting with an emotional behavior. In some cases the stimuli had, in reality, been responsible for the behavior. In other cases, the film had been spliced to associate inappropriate stimuli with emotional behavior. After viewing each film, the observers were asked to identify the emotional behavior they had just seen exhibited. Through this rather simple technique, Sherman demonstrated that observers were extremely variable in labeling emotional behaviors. More importantly, he showed that observers were unable correctly to identify emotional behavior when they were shown films depicting fallacious stimulus events. By using as observers students trained in a variety of disciplines, he demonstrated that training in psychology was no assist in correctly classifying emotional behavior.

It seems, however, that Sherman may have attacked Watson's theory on a false issue, for his research dealt simply with the verbal labeling by adults of infant emotional behavior. Although Sherman scored responses as correct and incorrect, he in no way demonstrated that he possessed any higher knowledge of "correctly" classifying the behaviors. A more pertinent criticism of Watson's work would seem to have been a demonstration of environmental control over the behaviors that Watson called "innate."

In 1920, 3 years after the publication of the Watson and Morgan paper, Watson and Rayner (1920) published the now famous case of "Little Albert." The intent of this research was to provide direct experimental evidence regarding the conditionability of human emotional behavior. The specific emotional behavior investigated was fear.

Albert B., the subject of this study, was a male infant who had been reared in a hospital environment almost from birth. Albert was 9 months of age at the start of the experiment and 13 months at the conclusion. He was characterized by Watson as being "stolid and unemotional" (Watson & Rayner, 1920, p. 1) at the outset of the experiment.

The experimental manipulation consisted of conditioning Albert to fear a white rat to which he had previously shown a neutral response. This conditioning process was done simply by repeatedly striking a steel bar a short distance behind Albert's head, while simultaneously presenting him with a white rat. Violent crying and attempts at withdrawal soon were noted in reaction to the rat alone.

After demonstrating that a fear response could be conditioned, Watson investigated the extent to which the fear generalized to similar objects. The results demonstrated that, upon being conditioned to fear the white rat, Albert displayed fearful reactions toward rabbits, dogs, and fur coats. Woolen balls and wooden blocks were test stimuli toward which Albert did not demonstrate fear.

Watson checked for the continuance of the conditioned fear after periods of 1 week and 31 days. In both instances, he found that the fear had persisted. Unfortunatedly, according to Watson, Albert left the hospital before his learned fears could be eliminated through reconditioning. Watson conjectured that the fears would persist indefinitely unless an accidental method for removing them was hit upon in the home.

Like the Watson and Morgan (1917) experiment discussed earlier, the Watson and Rayner (1920) investigation failed to provide any quantitative data. Obviously then, there was no attention to reliability of observations. Moreover, Watson implemented no method of control that would demonstrate that the fearful behaviors were functionally related to the experimental manipulations.

By 1926, Watson had refined his conditioning of laboratory-induced fear and of beginning to treat and modify fears that had been learned in the natural environment (Watson, 1926). Jones (1924), one of Watson's students, also conducted early work in the removal of children's naturally learned fears. She outlined several strategies found successful in the removal of fears. Although the jargon used was somewhat different, the techniques described by Jones—elimination through disuse and the method of negative adaption—were similar to the procedures used today in behavior therapy for the treatment of phobias (Kelly, 1973; Wolpe, 1969).

Goodenough (1931), through her research on children's anger, has added more data to the premise that emotional behaviors are learned and are subject to environmental control. After collecting substantial normative data on children's anger, she developed a chart that delineated the specific and immediate causes of anger in children of various age levels. Goodenough then identified the techniques which were commonly used by parents in attempts to control children's anger and contrasted these with more effective strategies found through research. Although it has been questioned whether or not the untrained observers (parents) used in Goodenough's research could distinguish between anger and fear (Valentine & Wickens, 1949), this point seems inconsequential since the research provided precise descriptions of emotional behaviors. Terms like "kicking," "stamping," "throwing self on floor," and "struggling" indicate clear behaviors. Whether these are labeled "fear" or "anger" is less important than the fact that they are representative of negative emotional behaviors.

Watson and the other pioneer behavioral investigators of emotion formulated an early attack on the problem of analyzing and treating emotional behavior. A distinctive characteristic of this work was its classical conditioning or respondent paradigm. It is interesting to note the impact of this early work on the respondent paradigm used in modern behavioral therapy. Wolpe (1969) has written that "behavior therapy had its conceptual origin in 1920 in Watson and Rayner's famous experiment on Little Albert" (p. 4). Wolpe has noted also that many current techniques of behavior therapy are based essentially on the early investigations of Watson and his associates. The collection of articles on behavior therapy edited by Franks (1969) has further reinforced the position that the respondent model of the early behavioral psychologists is widely applied in the practice of current behavioral therapy.

Social–emotional educators, like behavior therapists, have as their goal the treatment of emotional behavior. It seems, then, that they might profitably follow the lead of behavior therapists in considering the implications of this early behavioral research on their professional endeavors.

This pioneer research was of great significance in its "landmark" qualities. It was of particular value since it provided the first operational definitions of emotional behavior. In this sense, it represented an early attempt to objectify human emotion. Nevertheless, this research was much less sophisticated in its measurement, methodology, and design than the emotional behavior research that was to follow.

Research on Altruism and Helping Behavior

One aspect of emotional behavior having direct implications for social–emotional education is that of humanitarianism or altruism. Although it is often maintained that child behavior characterized by aiding others or sharing with peers is a goal of affective education (Rogers, 1969; Weinstein & Fantini, 1970), educators have yet to develop specific strategies for accountably teaching such behavior. There exist, however, several examples of empirical research that demonstrate control over sharing and altruistic behavior, and thus offer implications for education. Aronfreed (1968) has emphasized the importance of conditioning in the development of altruistic behavior. He also has suggested that, when children observe acts of charity or altruism and are made to understand that more desirable consequences result, they are likely to imitate the altruistic act. Byron (1971) has held that, if adults wish children to behave altruistically, they should demonstrate or "model" such behavior to the children. Byron (1971) has conducted research investigating the occurrence of altruistic modeling.

The subjects of this research were first- and second-grade children. The procedure of Byron's (1971) research involved presenting a "model" to the subjects via videotape. The model was portrayed playing a bowling game and "winning" pennies for his efforts. After receiving his reward, the model either demonstrated altruism by depositing a portion of the pennies in a March of Dimes canister or kept the entire reward for himsef. A poster suggesting contributions to the March of Dimes (supposedly within the comprehension range of the subjects) was placed in the experimental room at all times. As Byron expected, the viewing of the altruistic model increased the likelihood that the subjects would deposit coins in the canister.

It would seem that an oversight in Byron's research was a failure to attend to the reinforcement value of the pennies to the subjects. The pennies were never demonstrated as having reinforcement value since the bowling game was designed in such a way that the subjects had to "win." Moreover, there is no information provided concerning the socioeconomic level or reinforcement history of the subjects. It is possible, then, that the pennies were of little value to the subjects and, thus, conclusions about "altruism" were unfounded. These remarks are not meant to discredit the experiment, since the collection of any quantitative data on such a topic is laudable. The study does provide a valuable demonstration of learned sharing.

Another study of sharing behavior (Doland & Adelberg, 1967) sought to investigate differences in initial (previously learned) levels of sharing behavior and responsiveness to being trained to share among upper-middle-class and lower-class children. The authors reported that the study was prompted by the observation that children from a "favored environment" seemed more likely to share than children from an impoverished environment. They hypothesized that upper-middle-class children not only would demonstrate more spontaneous sharing behavior than lower-class children, but also would be more responsive to training procedures designed to encourage sharing.

The subjects of this research were 20 white upper-middle-class children attending a private nursery school and 16 predominately black lower-class children attending a child-welfare center. The mean age of both groups was 4 years, 6 months. The procedure of this experiment involved providing the children, in the context of a game, an opportunity to share either spontaneously or following training sessions. The game involved a match-to-sample task with pictures of animals. Sharing was defined as giving an animal picture that the subject needed in the performance of his matching task to a peer who apparently had a greater need for it. The peers with whom the pictures were shared, were actually confederates of the experimenters, or "plants." That is, they were children brought into the classroom by the experimenters for the purposes of the experiment. These confederates previously had been instructed in how to behave in the experimental setting. At the beginning of the experiment, the subjects were given neutral instructions concerning the value of the sharing behavior. If any subject demonstrated sharing behavior in this pretraining stage of the experiment, it was concluded that sharing was already a part of his repertoire, and his part in the study was completed. Failure to share the needed picture with the confederate was defined as a nonsharing behavior. If a subject did not share in the pretraining session, the experimenter returned 2 days later and engaged the subject in the animal-matching game again, but with a procedural modification designed to train sharing. On this occasion, the experimenter indicated clearly that the subject would receive "social reinforcement" if he engaged in sharing. The experimenter made statements like "I think it would be very nice if you shared your dogs with Jimmy. That would be the really nicest thing to do" (Doland & Adelberg, 1967, p. 697). If the subject shared at this stage of the training, his part in the study was completed. If not, the experimenter returned 2 days later and modified the game still further. On this occasion, the animal pictures were distributed so that the subject needed some of the pictures possessed by the confederate. As before, the confederate needed some of the pictures of the subject. Additionally, the experimenter had previously instructed the confederate to share his pictures with the subject. The experimenter indicated to the subject, in even stronger terms than before, that it would be desirable for him to share.

The results of this experiment were consistent with the expectations of the authors. Out of 20 of the upper-middle-class subjects, 10 shared in the pretraining session, whereas only 2 of the 16 lower-class children did so. This difference was significant on a chi-square analysis at the .05 level. Of the initial nonsharers, all 10 of the upper-middle-class children learned to share by the conclusion of the experiment, as compared with 9 of the 14 initial nonsharers from the lower-class group. The experimenters have reported that this difference was significant on the Fisher Exact Probability Test at the .05 level.

It would seem that the results of this experiment are consistent with an environmentalist perspective. Children from deprived environments would seem to be less likely to share their paucity of resources than children who had been reared in environments of plenty. However, there were some methodological errors in the study which could have swayed the results in the expected direction. First of all, the praise for sharing, defined by the authors as "social reinforcement" (Doland & Adelberg, 1967, p. 697), seemed to serve different functions in the two groups. Since the experimenters were white and middle class, it would be expected that their instructions would be differentially acted upon by upper-middle- and lower-class children. Secondly, the "planted peers" were also Caucasian. It would have seemed a more rigorous procedure to have used black confederates in the welfare center since the children there were predominantly black. Lower-class, black preschool children may have had little opportunity to interact with white children and therefore might be less apt to share with them. Additionally, there is no way of determining from the experiment whether or not the lower-class children would have learned to share under different training conditions or under extended training in the conditions actually employed. It is generally accepted that children of differing environmental histories respond differentially to similar contingencies. This conclusion, albeit unrecognized, is also discernible from the Doland and Adelbert (1967) study. Affective educators should be aware of this difference in children of varying reinforcement histories and therefore not attempt to apply the same educational tactics to all children.

A study by Presbie and Coiteax (1971) sought to investigate not only the effect on sharing of viewing a "generous model" but also the differential effects of viewing a "stingy model." The experimenters based their expectation that children viewing a "generous model" would share more than children viewing a "stingy model" on the social-learning theory of Bandura and Walters (1963). Additionally, the experiment investigated the effects of experimenter praise of a model and self-praise of a model on the observational learning of a subject viewing the model.

In this study, 64 first-grade children were placed at random in stingy or generous model conditions. These groups were subdivided so that the subjects heard the experimenter praise the model, the model praise himself, or no praise at all. The subjects first observed the experimenter instruct a model to divide a bag of 12 marbles between himself and a "sharee." The "stingy" model gave 3 marbles to the sharee while keeping 9 for himself, while the "generous" model gave 9 to the sharee and kept 3. The model was praised by the experimenter, by himself, or received no praise, in accordance with the experimental treatment in effect. After the model had distributed the marbles, he left the room and the subject was instructed to divide the marbles.

The results indicated that the subjects who had observed the generous model gave significantly more marbles to the "sharee" (repeated measures ANOVA, $F = 76.38$, $p. < 001$). The mean number of marbles given to the sharee was 8.04 and 4.56, for the generous and stingy model conditions respectively. The experimenters were surprised to find, however, that neither praise condition differentially affected the amount shared. Additionally, there were no differences in sharing behavior as a function of sex.

In contrast to the Byron (1971) study previously reviewed, wherein the subjects observed a model share or not share, the Presbie and Coiteax (1971) study demonstrated that training procedures can affect not only the existence of sharing behavior but also the degree of such behavior.

Affective educators should attend with interest to such studies since the method employed seems to offer a successful technique for teaching children to share. It seems that a logical extension of this study which would be appropriate for a researcher in emotional education might be to train children to share using the laboratory technique employed here, and subsequently observe the amount of sharing demonstrated by the trained children in the natural environment of the classroom. The goal of such research would be to delineate setting events in a natural environment which would result in sharing behavior. Even more generalizable, however, would be the development of classroom teaching strategies that resulted in increased levels of sharing among children. For emotional education to become most efficacious, the training should occur in an environment as natural as possible.

Severy and Davis (1971) have made beginning steps in researching "helping behavior" in classroom settings. This study was descriptive and, as such, did not involve any experimental manipulations. Rather, the experimenters sought to compare the naturally occurring helping behaviors among normal and retarded children. The subjects of this study were of 2 C.A. groups, from 3 to 5 and from 8 to 10. Each C.A. group contained one group of retarded subjects and one group of normals. The retarded subjects were from a special day-care center, and their mean IQ equalled 56. The normal subjects were from a university preschool, but IQ scores were unreported. All data were collected during free play time.

A particularly noteworthy aspect of this study was an intricate behavior-coding system developed by the experimenters which provided highly reliable data on a number of helping behaviors. The behavioral categories and the levels of reliability obtained for each between independent observers were as follows: *psychological help*—shows concern (.99); advises, suggests, and interprets

(.90); comforts and reassures (.90); *task help*—fixes (.99); protects, warns and defends (.90); gets help for (1.00); helps accomplish task (.75); helps out of distress (.90).

Unfortunately, the experimenters did not specify their actual observational methodology. They simply indicated that the data for each subject were composed of observed frequencies of the behaviors listed earlier. That oversight notwithstanding, the kinds of behavior-coding categories developed by these experimenters would seem to be of use to affective educators. The behaviors coded in this system are often stated goals of affective education, but to date no one in the field has gathered systematic data on such behaviors.

The results of this study (Severy & Davis, 1971) revealed a consistent interaction effect in which all indices of helping behavior increased with age in the retarded subjects, but decreased or showed no change among the normals. It was also observed, though not empirically demonstrated, that frequencies of helping behavior varied as a function of opportunities available for such behavior.

As a study of helping behavior this experiment offered the innovation of being conducted in "natural" settings. Moreover, the observational-coding system used in this experiment is seen as a potential contribution of emotional education. It seems, however, that the experimenters are methodologically in error when they attribute the differences in helping behavior to C.A. and mental retardation. Although the authors acknowledge that helping behavior seems to vary partially as a function of the number of opportunities for its occurrence, they fail to perceive that these opportunities were no doubt unequivalent in the two setttings where data were gathered. Modification is needed in future research design to control for the effects of differential opportunities to behave which are available across settings.

It should be pointed out that Macaulay and Berkowitz (1970) have edited a book of theoretical and empirical articles on the subject of altruism and helping behavior. Most of the writing and experiments contained in this book, however, are oriented to a rather phenomonological framework which would be difficult or impossible to translate into accountable educational methods. Most of the research on altruism and helping behavior included in the present review was selected on the basis of its focus on observable social–emotional behaviors and its de-emphasis of more theoretical orientations. Since such research has revealed that sharing and altruistic behaviors are systematically tractable, the methods and procedures employed should be of value to social–emotional educators seeking accountable techniques of training.

Research on Affectional and Aggressive Behavior

Many studies have investigated the occurrence (Walters, Pearce, & Dahms, 1959) and the learned nature (Brackbill, 1958; Hopkins, 1968; Lovaas, Schaeffer, & Simmons, 1965; Williams, 1959; Zelazo, 1971) of a variety of affectional and aggressive emotional behaviors in children.

Walters and his associates (1959) have researched the development of affection and aggression. Their study bears significant relevance to social–emotional education due to the nature of the investigated behaviors as well as to the behavior coding system utilized by the experimenters. The objectives of this study were to compare across age and sex: (a) the number of affectional and aggressive responses demonstrated during free play in a nursery school setting, (b) the frequency with which young children initiate social contact by means of affectional or aggressive behavior, and (c) the individuals (adults, boys, or girls) chosen recipients of such affectional or aggressive contact.

Affectional behavior was defined in this study as "behavior directed towards another person which indicated warm regard, friendliness, sympathy, or helpfulness" (Walters et al., 1959, p. 15) and was subdivided into 11 operationally defined behaviors. Aggressive behavior was defined as "an actual attack or theoretical attack upon another person, whether it be by gesture or hostile or provocative language" (Walters et al., 1959, p. 15) and was subdivided into 18 operationally defined behaviors.

The subjects were 124 children attending a university kindergarten. They were divided by C.A.; 2-year-olds, 3-year-olds, 4-year-olds, and 5-year-olds. The methodology used in this study was a direct observation system employing predetermined behavioral categories and a time-sampling technique. The experimenters devised several behavioral coding systems before developing the sophisticated one used in the study. The final instrument contained 11 affectional and 18 aggressive categories. Due to the perceived relevance of these behavioral categories to affective education, they are listed here.

Physical affection: This overall category contained six subcategories as follows.

1. Compliant, that is, conforms to another's desire on request
2. Kisses
3. Hugs
4. Smiles, laughs with someone
5. Helpful, shares, that is, gives assistance to another, divides materials with others
6. Sympathetic

Verbal affection: This overall category contained five subcategories as follows.

1. Accepts, that is, receives with favor, approves
2. Asks permission, requests
3. Speaks in a friendly manner, that is, talks with another in such a manner so as to reassure, to express warm feelings to the person
4. Compliments, praises
5. Offers to compromise, cooperate

Physical aggression: This overall category contained eight subcategories as follows.

1. Annoys, teases, interferes
2. Hits, strikes
3. Competes for status, that is, attempts to "show up" another by performing better
4. Threatening gesture
5. Pursues, that is, runs after or follows with the intent of inflicting a blow
6. Snatches or damages property of others
7. Negativism, that is, refuses to work with, or conform to directions of another
8. Pushes, pulls, holds

Verbal aggression: This overall category contained ten subcategories as follows.

1. Commands, demands

2. Cross purposes, that is, conflict over ways of using equipment
3. Disparages, that is, makes remark indicating dislike for another person, finds fault with or censures or condemns another's behavior, humiliates, laughs at another's misfortune; mocks, expresses desire that another be the victim of impervious events, attributes bad qualities to another
4. Injury via agent, that is, entices another person to injure a third person
5. Refuses to comply
6. Rejects, that is, denies activity or privilege to another
7. Shifts blame
8. Tattles
9. Claims possession
10. Threatens

These behavioral categories appeared on a check list. Any affectional or aggressive behaviors which a child demonstrated in a given one minute interval were recorded by checking the appropriate categories. A total of 40 1-minute observations were made on each of the 124 subjects. This descriptive data, then, represented the results of this study. All data were recorded during "self-directed activity" time. The observers stayed in sufficient physical proximity to the target subject at all times to overhear his conversation.

In spite of the judgmental nature of some of the behavior categories used in this study, the experimenters were successful in training three independent observers to acheive a mean reliability level across categories of behavior of .85. This coefficient represents the mean percentage of agreements. The fact that the experimenters report a mean level of reliability obviously indicates that there was variability in values across categories. Unfortunately, reliability scores are not given for individual categories of behavior. The major findings of this study were as follows.

1. Children of three, four, and five were more verbally than physically affectionate.
2. There was no difference in frequency of physical and verbal aggression.
3. Aggression increased with age from two to four.
4. Boys were more aggressive than girls.

5. At all age levels children were more often affectionate than aggressive.
6. At the 2-, 3-, and 4-year-old levels the boys initiated more affectionate behaviors with boys than with girls, while the 2-year-old girls were more often affectionate toward girls than toward boys.
7. There was a tendency for boys of all age levels to use other boys or adults rather than girls as recipients of their affectionate behavior.
8. The boys of all age groups were more likely to display aggressive behaviors to other boys than to adults.

This study has offered many implications for affective education. Of primary importance was the development of the reliable behavioral checklist which delineated 29 social–emotional or affective behaviors. This objective and reliable checklist seems to be precisely the kind of tool needed by affective educators to begin to operationalize their field. Although Walters *et al.* (1959) used their checklist in descriptive research, there is no reason such an instrument could not be used as a measurement device in emotional-behavior research involving the manipulation of variables. It would be interesting, for example, to gather baseline data using the instrument described and then assess various experimental techniques in affective education by gathering "process" and "product" data with the checklist across educational techniques.

It also should be kept in mind that these researchers (Walters *et al.*, 1959) merely demonstrated the viability of one specific affective behavior checklist. It would seem appropriate for affective educators seeking measurement systems to use this instrument as a starting point and adapt it to their particular research or educational needs.

One microcosmic variety of affectional behavior that has been experimentally controlled is that of smiling. Smiling behavior in infants and children seems an important area of social–emotional development for several reasons. First of all, it is one of the initial modes of interaction by which an infant may develop social contact with his caretakers. Secondly, it seems likely that a child could attract positive adult attention with a friendly smile. That is, smiling may be a reinforcer for adults attending to children. Additionally, the smiling behavior of children may initiate a sequence of social interaction that could lead to the development of enhanced opportunities for social–emotional development.

It is now widely accepted that smiling in infants can be increased through the contingent application of positive reinforcement (Zelazo, 1971). Several derivations of this principle have been demonstrated.

A study of Brackbill (1958) sought to investigate the smiling behavior of infants as a function of reinforcement schedule. The subjects of Brackbill's research were eight normal infants between the ages of 3½ and 4½ months of age and of middle-class socioeconomic backgrounds. The subjects were randomly assigned to regularly reinforced or intermittently reinforced groups. The group termed "regularly reinforced" was actually on an FR 1 schedule. The group termed "intermittently reinforced" received reinforcement on an FR 1 schedule for the first 10 smiles, an FR 2 schedule for the next 60 smiles, an FR 3 schedule for the next 45 smiles, and an FR 4 schedule for the next 20 smiles. This scheduled leaning occurred over a period of several days since no more than 6 smiles could occur in any 5-minute experimental session, with 3 sessions occurring daily for each subject. The reinforcement for smiling was 45 seconds of close bodily contact between experimenter and subject, consisting of hugging, bouncing, jostling, and talking. Prior to each conditioning session, the infants were placed under conditions of social deprivation for 15 to 20 minutes. This meant that the subjects received no attention that was not necessary for their safety and well-being.

Data were collected also on "protest behaviors." Brackbill (1958) defined protest behaviors as "crying and fussing," and pointed out that these were the only aggressive behaviors of which an infant is capable.

The results of this study revealed that intermittent reinforcement was superior to continuous reinforcement for the maintenance of smiling behavior. Further, a significant negative correlation was found between "protest" and smiling behaviors under both reinforcement schedules. The experimenter concluded that smiling was not only a function of reinforcement but was also affected by the performance of incompatible behaviors. If Brackbill had utilized an individual rather than a group experimental design, she could have investigated more closely the functional relationship of smiling and "protest" behaviors to reinforcement. Rather, this experimenter dismissed the "protest" behaviors as "interfering," without any analysis of their operant nature. Moreover, although the smiling and "protest" behaviors investigated in this research would seem to be objectively countable, the experimenter did not consider reliability of observations.

Zelazo (1971) has conducted more recent research on smiling behavior in infants. The subjects of Zelazo's research were 20 infants between the ages of 11 and 13 weeks. All subjects were tested in their own homes. Zelazo gathered reliability data on smiling behavior and reported a mean interrater-reliability coefficient of .97. He did not report the computational system used in arriving at this value, however. Zelazo used hugging, jostling, and talking as reinforcement for smiling. An independent variable of interest in this experiment was the sex of the reinforcer. Data were collected three times per day for 6 days on each subject.

During the baseline stage of this experiment, the experimenter was "totally unresponsive" to any behaviors of the subjects. During conditioning, the experimenter reinforced the subject on an FR 1 schedule. The results (analyzed with ANOVA) indicated that smiling could be increased initially through contingent social reinforcement. Additionally, the subjects responded more quickly to male reinforcers than to female. Interestingly, however, the learned smiling declined to base rate about midway in the experiment. Unfortunately, the group design and the inferential statistical analysis used in this experiment were inadequate to explain this phenomenon. Had the experimenter implemented a design that permitted a more functional analysis of smiling and its relationship to "social reinforcement," the real meaning of the noted "habituation" effect may have become apparent.

An operant study of smiling behavior (Hopkins, 1968) has more closely analyzed the learned nature of this social–emotional behavior. The initial low rate of smiling in the two retarded subjects of this research was judged to contribute to deficiencies in other areas of social development. Hopkins (1968) has pointed out that previous commentators held such conditions as insufficient attention (Hurlock, 1964), or internal states like fear or anxiety (Jersild, 1954), responsible for aberrant emotional development. Such judgments concerning emotional behavior also seem to characterize affective educators (Henderson, 1970; Weinstein & Fantini, 1970).

Hopkins has successfully demonstrated, using a single-subject research design, that smiling is attributable to environmental manipulation that can increase or decrease its rate. This explanation is valuable to emotional educators in that it contains greater implications for treatment or education than do intrapsychic explanations.

This investigation consisted of two single-subject experiments. The first subject was a retarded (functioning level unspecified) 10-year-old boy attending a special day school. This child was reported to maintain typical facial expressions characterized as "pitiful," "sad," or "dejected." The smiling behavior investigated in this research was sufficiently well-defined to permit near-perfect reliability coefficients between independent observers. The procedures of this experiment involved walking with the subject around the grounds of the school and reinforcing him with candy, contingent on his smiling at people encountered. This tactic greatly increased the subject's rate of smiling. Ceasing to reinforce the smiling with candy, however, did not result in a lower rate of smiling. Hopkins reasoned that the smiling was then being reinforced by social interchange with the people encountered on the experimental walks. Therefore, the experimenter placed a sign on the subject designed to make social interaction with fellow pedestrians contingent on nonsmiling. This tactic was successful in lowering the rate of smiling. To complete the demonstration of experimental control and the operant nature of smiling, the experimenter changed the sign to call for social interaction contingent on smiling. As expected, this manipulation resulted in a marked increase of the behavior under investigation. When finally the sign was removed, the subject continued a high rate of smiling at the people encountered in his walks around the grounds.

The second subject of Hopkins' research (1968) was an 8-year-old retarded boy (functioning level unspecified) who was also judged to demonstrate an abnormally low rate of smiling. In fact, this child was never observed to smile during the baseline stage of the experiment. Following baseline, the experimenter instituted a "potential" contingency of candy for smiling. The experimenter did not, however, report any attempt to explain this contingency to the subject. No smiles were noted during this stage, and no candy was administered. In the next stage of the experiment, verbal instructions to smile administered to the subject increased smiling, but the effect did not maintain. At this point, however, the smiling would seem to have become part of the subject's repertoire since the re-establishment of the candy contingency (on a FR 1 schedule) resulted in an increased rate. When the candy reinforcement was discontinued, the rate of smiling decreased to near baseline level. Candy reinforcement was again reinstated on a FR 1 schedule of reinforcement and the behavior regained a normal level. The schedule of reinforcement was then progressively leaned to VR 1.25, VR 1.67, VR 2.5, VR 5, and finally VR 7.5. The smiling remained at a high level throughout the progressively leaned schedules, and even maintained when the candy reinforcer was discontinued entirely. The experimenter than attached a sign to the subject, making social interaction contingent on nonsmiling. This manipulation of social reinforcement resulted in a marked decrease in smiling. Modifying the sign to make social reinforcement contingent on smiling was successful in increasing the smiling again to its previously high rate.

The results of Hopkins' (1968) research have demonstrated that smiling is a learned and teachable behavior. Other operant researchers have exerted control over a variety of emotional behaviors. Whereas most operant investigators have sought to decrease undesirable emotional behaviors, Hopkins' work was unusual in that it focused on increasing a desirable emotional behavior. An experiment by Williams (1959) is fairly representative of much operant research on emotional behavior.

The subject of Williams' research was a 21-month-old male infant. The experimenter reported that the child demonstrated aggressive tantrum behavior in order to control the behavior of his parents. This form of negative emotional behavior was especially noted at the child's bedtime, when he was frequently unwilling to retire at an appropriate hour without inordinate amounts of adult attention being paid to him.

Upon investigation, Williams found no medical explanation for the subject's tantrum behavior and therefore hypothesized that the behavior was an operant, reinforced through contingent adult attention. The technique for eliminating the undesirable behavior, then, appeared simple. Working in the home of the subject, the experimenter instructed the parents to begin putting him to bed with only an appropriate amount of attention accompanying the event. As expected, the subject initially screamed and cried following this decrease in parent attention. The experimenter timed the duration of the tantrum behavior from the moment the parents had exited from the child's bedroom until its termination.

As expected, the tantrum behavior decreased almost immediately when it was no longer consequented by parent attention. When an aunt of the subject, who was naive of the experimental treatment, assumed responsibility for putting him to bed, the tantrum behavior began again as the aunt consequented it with attention. When the aunt was instructed to ignore all episodes of such tantrums, the behavior again decreased dramatically.

The results of this experiment are held to demonstrate that aggressive tantrums, an emotional behavior often attributed to intrapsychic causes (Bettelheim, 1950), is, in reality, a learned behavior controlled by environmental contingencies. It should be noted that no undesirable side effects on the subject of Williams' (1959) experiment were noted. Two years after the experiment, the child was reported to be a friendly, expressive, outgoing child.

Affective educators should ponder such research and attend particularly to the reinforcement techniques used in treating emotional behaviors. An appropriate supplement to the tactics heretofore employed would seem to be the modification of some microcosmic emotional behavior, such as smiling, while gathering data on concomitant changes in more macrocosmic areas of behavior, such as "friendly" social interaction. Through such a method, emotional educators could determine the broader impact of some simple intervention.

It has been pointed out that most operant scientists investigating emotional behavior have directed their efforts toward the deceleration of undesirable behaviors. Positive reinforcement of some variety has typically been the training vehicle used in such research. The research of Lovaas and his colleagues (1965), then, is atypical in two respects. That is, Lovaas has accelerated desirable emotional behavior, but his techniques have included aversive conditioning. It should be pointed out at the outset of this discussion that Lovaas's two subjects were 5-year-old, "autistic like" children with whom all previous treatment attempts had failed. These children exhibited no appropriate social or emotional responsiveness. Additionally, neither speech nor appropriate play with objects was ever observed to be demonstrated by the subjects. Professional judgment indicated that these children would likely be institutionalized for life in the absence of any successful treatment.

In Lovaas' research (1965), shock was administered to the subjects by means of an electrified grid on the floor or by an electric device strapped to the buttocks of the subjects. The shock was administered contingent on emotionally pathological behaviors. It was withheld when the subject approached the adults who were present. "Thus, those adults 'saved' the children from a dangerous situation; they were the only 'safe' objects in a painful invironment" (Lovaas et al., 1965, p. 100).

The first experiment reported in the Lovaas et al. (1965) paper involved an initial pretraining or preshock condition which served as a baseline. The experimenters simply placed the subject in the experimental room and invited him to "come here" about five times each minute for 15 minutes. The observers recorded the amount of physical contact (defined as the subject touching an experimenter with his hands), self-stimulatory and tantrum behavior, the verbal commands "come here," and positive responses to the command (defined as the subject approaching to within 1 foot of the experimenter within 5 seconds of the command). Under the first shock, or training condition of the experiment, the experimenter would issue the invitation to "come here." If the subject did not approach, the shock was administered until the subject moved in the direction of the experimenter. If the subject did not approach within 3 seconds, he was "primed" by being pushed by an attendant in the direction of the experimenter. This training program was continued with the experimenter standing successively farther away from the subject. Using this technique, the subjects were successfully trained to approach adults on command. Lovaas utilized a reversal or ABAB design in the experiment to demonstrate the functional effect of the shock on the approach behavior of the subjects. Moreover, the application of shock contingent on self-destructive or tantrum behavior was successful in reducing such behaviors to a previously unobserved low rate.

In another experiment with the same subjects, Lovaas et al. (1965) was successful in training the subjects to demonstrate the affectional behaviors of embracing, hugging, and kissing. Lovaas utilized avoidance conditioning and a successive approximations technique in shaping the subjects from hesitant approaches to enthusiastic hugging and cuddling. To demonstrate the functional relationship between shock and the behavior, Lovaas again employed an ABAB or equivalent time sample design.

Of particular interest, although unsupported by behavioral data, is Lovaas' observation that the shock training seemed to have a generalized effect on the social behavior of the subjects. Lovaas has reported that the children seemed more alert, affectionate, and seeking of adult company after the training in appropriate social–emotional behavior.

It is probably not likely that those interested in emotional education would consider utilizing the technique of Lovaas. This research is included in the present review, however , to demonstrate that, even in cases of children initially devoid of social–emotional responsiveness, such behavior is teachable. Of course, the extreme methods used by Lovaas would be so unnecessary and inhumane if applied to normal children as to be unconsiderable. However, the need for techniques of emotional education for severely handicapped children has been noted (Bradtke et al., 1972). It should be kept in mind that the techniques used by Lovaas are, as yet, the only ones that have been proven to be effective in treating the emotional behavior of severely aberrant children. Educators responsible for such children apparently must choose between no effective training and aversive training with possible improvement implied. As Solomon (1964) has pointed out, this decision involves an ethical rather than a scientific judgment.

The collective findings of the research on affectional and aggressive behavior here reviewed indicate clearly that a variety of social–emotional behaviors can be reliably measured and effectively treated. Since such objective measurement and accountable intervention is a requisite for emotional education, it seems that affective educators ought to examine these research methodologies and findings and begin to translate them into educational-intervention procedures.

Research and Development in Affective Education

Although most of the research thus far reviewed as being relevant to emotional education has been conducted by experimental psychologists, educators also have contributed. Unfortunately, much of the education literature contains serious methodological flaws. Bradtke et al. (1972), for example, have reported on a technique they call "intensive play" as a strategy for building affective behaviors in profoundly retarded children. Although this article was presented as an empirical study, the methodology and results were reported in only the vaguest manner, lacking quantifiable data. Additionally, the authors failed to establish interrater reliability on the targeted affective behaviors, thus adding to the difficulty in evaluating the study.

Another educational study with similar flaws in methodology and design has been reported by Borich (1971). Borich has conducted research that included an attempt to operationalize Bloom's five behavioral distinctions in the affective domain (Krathwohl, Bloom, & Masia, 1964). Like the Bradtke et al. (1972) study, however, Borich's research lacked any attempt to establish reliability on the observed behaviors. Additionally, Borich conceded that changes in the affective behavior investigated could have been the result of factors other than those controlled for in the experimental design. Unfortunately, therefore, these data cannot be accepted by an emotional educator concerned with accountability or replication.

Other educational researchers (Rooze, 1969) have developed studies around Bloom's taxonomy. Unfortunately, methodological errors have also persisted in this research. Rooze (1969) has attempted to operationalize Bloom's taxonomy in the affective domain (Krathwohl et al., 1964) in reference to an evaluation system for the affective components of instructional materials. Rooze proposed to rate and compare instructional materials on a continuum modeled after Bloom's taxonomy. There were, however, at least two errors in this attempt which precluded its wide applicability. First of all, an interpretation of the materials was required in assigning them a place on the continuum. This interpretation was made by the author with no validity or reliability considerations reported. Secondly, the language used in the taxonomy was sufficiently nebulous to have divergent meanings to different readers. For example, it seems very subjective to maintain that a child is "valuing" an educational experience. In future work of this kind, the terms of the taxonomy should be operationally defined to have similar meaning to all readers.

A somewhat more rigorous educational study has been conducted by Anandam, Davis, and Poppen (1971). These investigators have conducted research comparing two techniques of affective education: "feelings classes" and "teacher reinforcement" of pupils' verbalizations concerning feelings. The subjects of this research were "normal" third-grade children. The subjects were randomly assigned to either a "feeling class" treatment condition or a treatment condition that involved teacher praise of verbalizations about feelings. The experimental treatment for the feelings classes involved a daily 1-hour feeling class. During these sessions, such activities as creative drawing and writing, small- and large-group "rap sssions," role playing, and confrontations were used in an attempt to promote the emotional growth of pupils. The second treatment condition involved the teacher instructing the children to verbalize their feelings. The teacher rewarded such behavior with verbal praise and a "feelings button." There were three classes of dependent variables in the study. First, the observable behaviors of working at a desk, directing attention to lessons, interaction with teacher, movement within the classroom, and off-task behavior were monitored. The second dependent variable was described as "children's self social construct" (Anandam et al., 1971, p. 183) and was measured with a paper and pencil test of the same name. The final dependent variable was "sociometric choice," defined as the peer to whom a subject passed a volleyball. Data were collected on the first dependent variable daily for each subject. Interrater reliability, defined as percentage of agreements between two independent observers, ranged between .86 and .92 for all observable behaviors comprising the first dependent variable. The second and third dependent variables were monitored as pre–post measures.

At the conclusion of the experiment, four significant differences were found in the observable-behavior dependent variable. The subjects in the teacher reinforcement group were found more often working at their desks. The subjects in the "feelings classes" were more likely to interact with the teacher, interact with peers and move about the classroom. All of these differences are consistent with what would be expected from an analysis of the contingencies operating in the two groups. The "feelings class" environment would seem to have promoted an "open classroom" kind of atmosphere, whereas the reinforcement class was a more traditional classroom arrangement.

The "self social construct" test did not reveal any significant differences on within-groups or between-groups comparison. Additionally, there were no differences found in sociometric choice.

The authors concluded that they had demonstrated two successful techniques of attending to children's feelings in a school setting. Since any substantial demonstration of experimental effect or control was lacking from the research, such claims seem presumptuous. Nevertheless, this research is seen as relevant as it represents initial steps in a hopefully growing movement to research empirically affective education. Future investigators in this area should attend more rigorously to the functional relationships between changes in emotional behavior and the emotional-education program employed.

Although the research reviewed thus far in this chapter is seen as having implications for, and applicability to, affective education, only a minority of the investigators have discussed such relationships directly. The scientists responsible for the bulk of research in emotional behavior have not described the relevance of their work to affective education. It seems that not only have emotional educators ignored research but also researchers have ignored emotional education. A group at the University of Massachusetts, however, has made tentative steps to combine the two disciplines. Alschuler and Ivey (1972) have attempted to use the principles and techniques of behavior analysis and modification to develop systematically positive affect in students in a natural environment. The goal of this program was to train students to be what are referred to by the developers as "intentional individuals" (Ivey, 1969, p. 36). An intentional individual has been defined as a person who has learned to increase rather than delimit available alternatives for behavior, and to act freely and spontaneously in response to his environment. Ivey (1969) has attempted to break their somewhat global ideals into specific behaviors. Some of these "specific behaviors" (as defined by Ivey) included: relaxation, decision making, combatting racism, and effective listening. Each behavior, in turn, was broken down into tractable units. Effective listening, for example, was subdivided as physical attention, verbal following, and eye contact (Alschuler & Ivey, 1972). In short, Alschuler and Ivey have attempted to develop a behavioral, performance-based, and accountable curriculum in social–emotional education. It is most unfortunate, therefore, that these affective educators have yet to publish comprehensive empirical reports that fully substantiate the claims of their training program. One data-based article published by this group (Ivey, Normington, Mills, Marvill, & Haase, 1969) was a report of an attempt to teach derivations of some of the "intentional individual" skills to counselor trainees. This research, however, did not focus on the observable behaviors that Ivey (1969) later identified. These writers (Alschuler & Ivey, 1972) do report, however, that they are currently engaged in behavioral research that they hope will demonstrate empirically the value of their training program in emotional education.

Some massive programs in emotional education have been undertaken without a reliance on empirical underpinnings. For example, the state of North Dakota has instituted what is possibly the largest scale attempt to redesign schools around affective educational goals. Madden (1972), in his writing on this project, has pointed out that those involved have found behavioral technology relevant and helpful to their task. After painful experience in trying to "free" North Dakota's children, Madden has discovered that this was not possible. Madden has written that, if a teacher refuses to exert control over children's behavior, the behavior simply will be controlled by other variables. Children come to school with a history of conditioning from previous school or authority interactions. This reinforcement history will control a child's behavior in an environment that attempts to exert no controls of its own. The behavioral norms the child has learned already will continue to be exhibited if no new norms are taught. Madden has concluded that to assume children are "free" in a humanistic school is a myth; human behavior always is controlled by environmental contingencies. In order to deal with control in a humanistic manner, then, the schools must strive for positive control based on positive reinforcement, and reject the aversive and punishing control tactics of the past. Thus, even Madden, a well-known "open school" advocate, has concluded that positive behavioral techniques offer the most efficacious method of developing the positive emotions of children.

Summary of Literature Review Findings and Their Implications for Behavioral Research in Social–Emotional Education

This review has considered the educational and psychological literature pertinent to the field of social–emotional education. The results of this review may be summarized in the following points.

1. The importance of social–emotional education in the total development of children has long been recognized (Prescott, 1938; Sandiford, 1936; Thorndike, 1906).
2. This area of need has been largely unmet by the educational institution (Beatty, 1969; Henderson, 1972; Hirschlein & Jones, 1971).
3. Criteria for widespread applicability of emotional education must include accountability, empirical validation, and objective measurement (Borich, 1971; Harbeck, 1970; Morse, 1971).
4. Existing models and curricula of emotional education have largely failed to meet the above criteria and have consequently been limited in scope and impact (Bradtke *et al.*, 1972; Ellis, 1971; Lyon, 1971).
5. Some experimental studies of children's emotional behavior and development have been conducted which offer implications to emotional education (Hopkins, 1968; Presbie & Coiteax, 1971; Walters *et al.*, 1959).
6. Research more directly relevant to emotional education is required to provide the field with the data base necessary for achieving accountability, objectivity, and replicability (Lyon, 1971; Morris, 1972).

Certain of the investigations reviewed in this chapter have built upon one another to point the direction to innovative and needed research. The pioneer investigators in emotional-behavior control (Goodenough, 1931; Watson & Morgan, 1917; Watson & Rayner, 1920) provided the first demonstrations of the learned nature of emotional behavior. Walters *et al.* (1959) demonstrated the feasibility of developing sophisticated observational systems that could reliably monitor operationally defined emotional behaviors. Brackbill (1958) demonstrated functional relationships between reinforcement schedules and smiling behavior. Hopkins (1968), Williams (1959), and Lovaas *et al.* (1965) utilized behavior-analytic reversal designs and together showed that both positive and negative emotional behavior could be increased and decreased through the contingent application of reinforcement techniques. Finally, Ascare and Axelrod (1973) have shown that behavioral techniques can be utilized to facilitate the attainment of emotional-education goals in a natural classroom environment.

Skinner (1948, 1953, 1972, 1974) has editorialized that behavioral techniques can be used to program environments in which cooperation, friendship, and peace prevail. Other behaviorists (O'Leary & O'Leary, 1972) have written that if, in the future, educators decide to emphasize affective, rather than cognitive growth, the procedures and techniques of applied behavior analysis would be the most efficacious approach to utilize. Homme (1970) has written of the importance of applying behavioral techniques to teach children to know joy and love. Lazarus (1973) has bemoaned the fact that behaviorists have heretofore not applied their discipline to teach people "how to emit forthright expressions of love, adoration, affection, appreciation and the specific verbal and nonverbal facets of compassion, tenderness, warmth, and other positive feelings" (p. 698).

In the remaining two chapters, we will discuss in detail the potential of operant psychology as a vital force in teaching social–emotional behaviors.

REFERENCES

Alschuler, A. S., & Ivey, A. E. The human side of competency based education. *Educational Technology,* 1972, *12,* 53–55.
Anandam, K., Davis, M., & Poppen, W. A. Feelings . . . to fear or to free? *Elementary School Guidance and Counseling,* 1971, *5,* 181–189.
Arnold, M. *Feelings and emotions.* New York: Academic Press, 1970.
Aronfreed, J. *Conduct and conscience: The socialization of internalized control over behavior.* New York: Academic Press, 1968.
Ascare, D., & Axelrod, S. Use of behavior modification in four "open" classrooms. *Psychology in the Schools,* 1973, *10,* 242–248.
Athey, I. J., & Rubadeau, D. O. *Educational implications of Piaget's theory.* Boston: Ginn-Blaisdell, 1970.
Axline, V. M. *Play therapy.* Boston: Houghton, 1947.
Baer, D. M., Wolf, M. M., & Risley, T. R. Some current dimensions of applied behavior analysis. *Journal of Applied Behavior Analysis,* 1968, *1,* 91–97.
Bandura, A. *Principles of behavior modification.* New York: Holt, 1969.
Bandura, A., & Walters, R. H. *Social learning and personality development.* New York: Holt, 1963.
Beatty, W. H. Emotions: The missing link in education. *Theory into Practice,* 1969, *8,* 86–92.
Bettleheim, B. *Love is not enough.* Glencoe, Illinois: Free Press, 1950.
Bijou, S. W., & Baer, D. M. *Child development: A systematic and empirical theory.* New York: Appleton, 1961.
Bijou, S. W., & Baer, D. M. *Child development II.* New York: Appleton, 1965.

Bijou, S. W., Peterson, R. J., Harris, F. R., Allen, K. E., & Johnson, M. S. Methodology for experimental studies of young children in natural settings. *Psychological Record,* 1969, *19,* 177–210.

Blatz, W. E. The cardiac, respiratory and electrical phenomena in the emotion of fear. *Journal of Experimental Psychology,* 1923, *8,* 109–132.

Borich, G. D. Accountability in the affective domain. *Journal of Research and Development in Education,* 1971, *5,* 87–96.

Brackbill, Y. Extinction of the smiling response in infants as a function of reinforcement schedule. *Child Development,* 1958, *29,* 115–124.

Bradtke, L. M., Kirkpatrick, W. J., & Rosenblatt, K. P. Intensive play: A technique for building affective behaviors in profoundly mentally retarded young children. *Education and Training of the Mentally Retarded,* 1972, *7,* 8–13.

Brill, A. A. (Ed.) *The basic writings of Sigmund Freud.* New York: Modern Library, 1938.

Byron, J. H. Model affect in children's imitative altruism. *Child Development,* 1971, *42,* 2061–2065.

Cartwright, C. A., & Cartwright, G. P. *Developing ovservational skills.* New York: McGraw-Hill, 1974.

Coles, R. *Erik H. Erickson: The growth of his work.* Boston: Little, Brown, 1970.

Day, W. F. Radical behaviorism in reconciliation with phenomonology. *Journal of the Experimental Analysis of Behavior,* 1969, *12,* 315–328.

Doland, D. J., & Adelberg, K. The learning of sharing behavior. *Child Development,* 1967, *38,* 695–700.

Ellis, A. An experiment in emotional education. *Educational Technology,* 1971, *11,* 61–64.

Erickson, E. *Activity and the life cycle.* New York: International Universities Press, 1959.

Franks, C. M. *Behavior therapy: Appraisal and status.* New York: McGraw-Hill, 1969.

Freud, A. *The psychoanalytic study of the child.* New York: International Universities Press, 1954.

Gesell, A., & Amatruda, C. *The embryology of behavior.* New York: Harper, 1945.

Goodenough, F. *Anger in young children.* Minneapolis: Univ. of Minnesota Press, 1931.

Gregg, D. B. Key to effective behavior. *Journal of Teacher Education,* 1971, *22,* 464–468.

Harbeck, M. B. Instructional objectives in the affective domain. *Educational Technology,* 1970, *10,* 49–52.

Henderson, L. A. A review of the literature on affective education. *Contemporary Education,* 1972, *44,* 92–99.

Hirschlein, B. M., & Jones, J. G. The function of stated objectives in teaching for affective learning. *Educational Technology,* 1971, *11,* 47–49.

Homme, L. E. Contingency contracting with parents. In *Proceedings: Early childhood intervention research conference.* Institute III: Exceptional Children and Adults. Tampa: Univ. of South Florida, 1970.

Homme, L., Csanyi, A., Gonzales, M., & Rechs, J. *How to use contingency contracting in the classroom.* Champaign, Illinois: Research Press, 1969.

Hopkins, B. L. Effects of candy and social reinforcement, instructions and reinforcement schedule leaning to the modification and maintenance of smiling. *Journal of Applied Behavior Analysis*, 1968, *1*, 121–129.

Hurlock, E. B. *Child development.* New York: McGraw-Hill, 1964.

Ivey, A. E. The intentional individual: A process-outcome view of behavioral psychology. *Counseling Psychologist*, 1969, *1*, 56–60.

Ivey, A. E., Normington, C. J., Miller, C. A., Marvill, W. H., & Haase, R. F. Microcounseling and attending behavior. *Journal of Counseling Psychology*, 1969, *15*, 1–12.

Jersild, A. L. Emotional development. In Carmichael (Ed.), *Manual of child psychology.* New York: Wiley, 1954. Pp. 833–917.

Jones, M. C. The elimination of children's fears. *Journal of Experimental Psychology*, 1924, *7*, 382–390.

Jones, R. M. *An application of psychoanalysis to education.* Springfield, Illinois: Charles C. Thomas, 1960.

Kazdin, A. E., & Bootzin, R. R. The token economy: An evaluative review. *Journal of Applied Behavior Analysis*, 1972, *5*, 343–372.

Kelly, E. W. School phobia: A review of theory and treatment. *Psychology in the Schools*, 1973, *10*, 32–42.

Kohlberg, L., & Mayer, R. Development as the aim of education. *Harvard Educational Review*, 1972, *42*, 449–456.

Krathwohl, A. R., Bloom, B. S., & Masia, B. B. *Taxonomy of educational objectives, Handbook II: Affective domain.* New York: David McKay, 1964.

Lazarus, A. A. On assertive behavior: A brief note. *Behavior Therapy*, 1973, *4*, 697–699.

Lovaas, O. I., Schaeffer, B., & Simmons, J. Q. Building social behavior in autistic children by use of electric shock. *Journal of Experimental Research in Personality*, 1965, *1*, 99–104.

Lyon, H. C. *Learning to feel—feeling to learn.* Columbus, Ohio: Charles E. Merrill, 1971.

Macauley, J., & Berkowitz, L. (Eds.) *Altruism and helping behavior.* New York: Academic Press, 1970.

Madden, P. C. Skinner and the open classroom. *School Review*, 1972, *81*, 100–107.

Maier, H. W. *Three theories of child development.* New York: Harper, 1965.

Marx, M. H., & Hillix, W. A. *Systems and theories in psychology.* New York: McGraw-Hill, 1963.

McClelland, D. C. Test for competence rather than for "intelligence." *American Psychologist*, 1973, *28*, 1–14.

Meacham, M. I., & Wiesen, A. E. *Changing classroom behavior: A manual for precision teaching.* Scranton, Pennsylvania: International Textbook, 1969.

Morris, J. E. School accountability and the affective domain. *School & Society*, 1972, *100*, 228–230.

Morse, W. C. Special pupils in regular classes: Problems of accommodation. In M. C. Reynolds & M. D. Davis (Eds.), *Exceptional children in regular classrooms.* Washington, D.C.: U.S. Office of Education, 1971.

Munroe, R. L. *Schools of psychoanalytic thought.* New York: Dryden Press, 1955.

O'Leary, K. D., & O'Leary, S. G. *Classroom management: The successful use of behavior modification.* New York: Pergamon Press, 1972.

Peters, R. S. The education of the emotions. In M. B. Arnold (Ed.), *Feelings and emotions: The Loyola symposium.* New York: Academic Press, 1970.

Piaget, J. *The moral judgment of the child.* Glencoe, Illinois: Free Press, 1948.

Piaget, J., & Inhelder, B. *The psychology of the child.* New York: Basic Books, 1969.

Popham, W. J. *Criterion referenced measurement.* Englewood Cliffs, New Jersey: Educational Technology Publications, 1971.

Presbie, R. J., & Coiteax, P. F. Training to be generous or stingy: Imitation of sharing behavior as a function of model generosity and vicarious reinforcement. *Child Development,* 1971, *42,* 1033–1038.

Prescott, D. A. *Emotion and the educative process.* Washington, D.C.: American Council on Education, 1938.

Reynolds, G. S. *A primer of operant conditioning.* Glenview, Illinois: Scott Foresman, 1968.

Ripple, R., & Rockcastle, V.N. (Eds.) *Piaget rediscovered: A report of the conference on cognitive studies and curriculum development.* A report of the Jean Piaget Conference at Cornell Univ. and the Univ. of California, March, 1964.

Rogers, C. R. *Freedom to learn.* Columbus, Ohio: Charles E. Merrill, 1969.

Rogers, C. *On encounter groups.* New York: Harper, 1970.

Rogers, C. R., & Skinner, B. F. Some issues concerning the control of human behavior: A symposium. *Science,* 1956, *124,* 1057–1066.

Rooze, G. E. Empirical evaluation of instructional materials in the affective domain. *Educational Technology,* 1969, *9,* 53–56.

Sandiford, P. *Educational psychology: An objective study.* New York: Longmans, Green, 1936.

Schrag, F. Learning what one feels and enlarging the range of one's feelings. *Educational Theory,* 1972, *22,* 382–394.

Sear, R. R., Maccoby, E. E., & Levin, H. *Patterns of child rearing.* Evanston, Illinois: Row Peterson, 1957.

Severy, L. J., & Davis, K. E. Helping behavior among normal and retarded children. *Child Development,* 1971, *42,* 1017–1031.

Sherman, M. The differentiation of emotional responses in infants. *Journal of Comparative Psychology,* 1927, *7,* 265–284.

Sidman, M. *Tactics of scientific research.* New York: Basic Books, 1960.

Skinner, B. F. *Walden two.* New York: Macmillan, 1948.

Skinner, B. F. *Science and human behavior.* New York: Free Press, 1953.

Skinner, B. F. *Contingencies of reinforcement.* New York: Appleton, 1972.

Skinner, B. F. *About behaviorism.* New York: Knopf, 1974.

Solomon, R. L. Punishment. *American Psychologist,* 1964, *19,* 239–253.

Thompson, R. F. *Foundations of physiological psychology.* New York: Harper, 1967.

Thorndike, E. *The principles of teaching.* New York: A. G. Seller, 1906.

Ulrich, R., Stachnik, T., & Mabry, J. (Eds.) *Control of human behavior.* Glenview, Illinois: Scott Foresman, 1970.

Valentine, W. L., & Wickens, D. D. *Experimental foundations of general psychology.* New York: Holt, 1949.

Wallace, G., & Kauffman, J. M. *Teaching children with learning problems.* Columbus, Ohio: Charles E. Merrill, 1973.

Walters, J., Pearce, D., & Dahms, L. Affectional and aggressive behavior of preschool children. *Child Development,* 1959, *28,* 15–26.

Watson, J. B. Recent experiments in how we lose and change our emotional equipment. In C. Murchoson (Ed.), *Psychologists of 1925*. Worcester, Massachusetts: Clark Univ. Press, 1926.

Watson, J. B., & Morgan, J. J. B. Emotional reactions and psychological experimentation. *American Journal of Psychology*, 1917, *28*, 163–174.

Watson, J. B., & Rayner, R. Conditioned emotional reactions. *Journal of Experimental Psychology*, 1920, *3*, 1–14.

Weinstein, G., & Fantini, M. D. *Toward humanistic education: A curriculum of affect*. New York: Praeger, 1970.

Williams, C. D. The elimination of tantrum behavior by extinction procedures. *Journal of Abnormal and Social Psychology*, 1959, *59*, 269.

Winnett, R. A., & Winkler, R. C. Current behavior modification in the classroom: Be still, be quiet, be docile. *Journal of Applied Behavior Analysis*, 1972, *5*, 499–504.

Wolpe, J. *The practice of behavior therapy*. New York: Pergamon Press, 1969.

Zelazo, P. Smiling to social stimuli. *Developmental Psychology*, 1971, *4*, 32–45.

Introduction

In the preceding chapter, we suggested that the operant-learning approach to conceptualizing and studying the social behavior of exceptional and normal children is a method that holds great potential for intervening successfully with delayed or deviant social-behavior patterns. There are, however, a number of critical measurement concerns that have not been met satisfactorily within the operant paradigm.

Since the early part of this century, the interaction of young children with peers and adults has been the subject of extensive experimental and naturalistic investigation. The analytic and normative information obtained from these studies subsequently has provided the research base for a number of theoretical accounts of the ontogeny and function of human social behavior (e.g., Bijou & Baer, 1965; Blurton Jones, 1972). The major reviews of literature on children's social encounters (Adams, 1967; Arrington, 1943; Hartup, 1970; Swift, 1964) have been complete and exacting in their critique of conceptual and methodological weaknesses. What has not been accounted for, however, is the relationship between theories of social behavior and the functional characteristics of the unit of measurement, or dependent variable employed in social behavior research.

It is proposed in this chapter that each of the major conceptualizations of social behavior (e.g., social drive–social reinforcement, dyadic interactional, and ethological) has produced distinctive, nonoverlapping research questions and idiosyncratic methodologies that produce data congruent with their particular theoretical constructs. A critical review will be made of the validity and generalizability of several behavioral and motivational constructs utilized by these theoretical positions. In examining the explanatory adequacy of these positions, particular emphasis is given to experimental procedures and the unit of measurement employed. Finally, specific behavioral and motivational constructs that have been used in observational systems for assessing interactions of young children will be discussed.

This review is intended to demonstrate the pervasive influence of inadequate theoretical constructs upon the selection of "relevant" behaviors in the study of social interaction. A second purpose is to provide a synthesis of those theoretical constructs and observational strategies that together can provide a comprehensive view of the development, maintenance, and function of children's interactive behavior.

Social Drive–Social Reinforcement Conceptualizations

The extension of learning–theory approaches to social behavior and development has its origins in the work of Dollard and Miller (1950), Miller and Dollard (1941), Mowrer (1950), Rotter (1954), and Skinner (1953),. With the exception of Skinner (1953), these learning-theory approaches have consisted largely of modifications of Freudian principles and concepts, such as the pleasure principle, ego strength, repression, and transference, into terms more commensurate with experimental psychology (Bandura & Walters, 1963).

Today, the most widely accepted learning–theory accounts of social behavior are based on the operant or Skinnerian framework, which has its social-learning beginnings in the efforts of Gewirtz and his coworkers, and the social-learning theory of Bandura and Walters. Although the research tactics and conceptualizations of the experimental analysis of behavior are antithetical to any study of nonobservables (e.g., drive states, intrapsychic motivation), the historical application of operant methodology to social behavior, like its learning-theory forerunners, has preserved a number of ambiguous, nonobservable, and restrictive constructs regarding the development of social behavior in children. For the purposes of this chapter, the discussion of operant psychology as applied by Gewirtz, Bandura and Walters, and others to problems of social behavior will focus upon the assumptions underlying the social drive–social reinforcement perspective, and how such an outlook has led to a highly stylized and limited method of observing and analyzing social interaction.

GEWIRTZ–BAER OPERANT TRADITION

A vast amount of experimental data has been collected regarding the operation of socially mediated contingencies of reinforcement on child behavior (see Eisenberger, 1970; Parton & Ross, 1965; Stevenson, 1965). As developed by Gewirtz and Baer (1958a), the aim of this research was to determine whether or not there are social drives that function in a manner similar to the primary appetitive drives. As such, the motivational, social-drive hypothesis is operationally identical to Miller's (1941) Freudian-based frustration–aggression hypothesis or other analyses that impute intrapsychic constructs as causal agents for observed social behavior.

Before reviewing the findings of this research, the methodology employed by these investigators will be examined. The principle task employed by Gewirtz and Baer was a simple marble-dropping game in which the child places marbles into the holes of a wooden box or bin. The child's rate of responding, or his persistence at the game under different conditions of social reinforcement, is assessed. In another variation, a two-choice discrimination task is employed and the child is given social approval for choosing the hole that is designated by the experimenter as "correct." The increase in the frequency of the correct response (preference-change score) is the index of social reinforcer effectiveness. As Stevenson (1965) has noted in his review of social reinforcement, a variety of factors governed the choice of this laboratory task. The marble-dropping game possesses little intrinsic interest and thereby maximizes the effects of social reinforcement. It minimizes the effects of earlier learning and so reduces the impact of individual differences on task performance. Moreover, the game involves discrete responses that can be measured readily in laboratory settings. Clearly, the methodology is highly congruous with Skinner's (1953) conceptualization of social behavior as an individual's discrete response that is under stimulus control mediated by another person. Considering the response topography measured here and the context in which it is evoked, the aim of the Gewirtz–Baer research may be restated in reference to determining the function of social reinforcers as they affect a *nonsocial* motor act.

In one study by Gewirtz and Baer (1958b), using nursery school children, responsiveness to verbal approval was compared either immediately upon the subject's entry into the experimental room or following 20 minutes of social isolation. Subjects initially were given an adaptation session, in order to familiarize them with the experimenter and the experimental task. In the social-isolation condition, subjects were left alone with playthings, having been told that the wait was necessary because the experimenter needed some time to repair a toy with which the subject was subsequently to play. During the test period, subjects dropped marbles into a wooden box through two holes. The marbles, six in total, fell into a tray from which they would be retrieved by the subject for reuse. The first portion of the test consisted of a baseline period, during which no verbal approval was dispensed. After the rate of marble dropping had become relatively stable (typically within 4 minutes), a 10-minute conditioning period ensued in which dropping marbles into one of the holes (the less frequently used during the last minute of the baseline period) was reinforced by approval comments according to an increasing fixed-ratio schedule. Each subject's preference-change score was computed for each minute of the conditioning period. The obtained difference score was taken as a measure of the reinforcement efficacy of verbal approval. As predicted, social isolation led to significantly better performance than nonisolation. The authors concluded that the findings provided evidence for the existence of a deprivation–satiation function for social approval. Gewirtz and Baer also proposed that approval comments were representative of the reinforcers that typically control the social initiations made by children to adults. They recognized, however, that social isolation (as operationalized here) involves deprivation of various social stimuli besides approval, and that further verification would require social stimulation other than approval during the deprivation period.

A second experiment (Gewirtz & Baer, 1958a), using second graders, included a third condition which was designed to afford initial satiation for verbal approval. Subjects received approximately 30 presentations of praise and admiration for whatever they said about themselves during an initial 20-minute conversation with the experimenter. Unlike the first experiment, there was no initial adaptation session. Subjects in the isolation condition were told that their wait was necessitated by someone else's using the game. As predicted, isolation subjects showed the greatest preference-change, followed in order by nondeprivation and satiation subjects.

As Eisenberger (1970) noted, the Gewirtz–Baer findings have been consistently replicated in a large number of studies employing choice measures of approval-contingent performance (e.g., Cohen, Greenbaum, & Mansson, 1963; Endo, 1968; Gewirtz, 1969; Hartup, 1958; Kozma, 1969; Landau & Gewirtz, 1967; Lewis, 1965; Lewis & Rachman, 1964). There are, however, serious methodological problems with this line of research, which make these results somewhat ambiguous.

Certainly the most forceful and effective criticism of the Gewirtz–Baer methodology was made by Parton and Ross (1965, 1967). In their review of studies concerned with the social reinforcement of children's motor behavior, Parton and Ross (1965) enumerated the deficiencies of the empirical indices used to measure social reinforcer effectiveness. Of particular concern to the present discussion are those assumptions regarding subject and experimental condition variables which are considered problematic .

The index of the presumed effect of social reinforcement introduced by Gewirtz and Baer (1958b), the preference ration, represents the number of responses to the less-preferred hole (Xb) divided by the total number of responses to both holes ($Xb + Yb$) during the last minute of a 4-minute nonreinforcement baseline period. A comparable preference ratio ($Xr/Xr + Yr$) is obtained for the reinforcement period or for several intervals within this period. In this ratio, Xr represents the number of responses to the hole that had been less preferred during the baseline period, and is, thus, the hole to which responses were reinforced during the experimental period. The difference between the values ($Xr/Xr + Yr$) and ($Xb/Xb + Yb$) is a preference-change score. As Parton and Ross (1965) suggest,

> this scoring system entails the questionable assumption that the base-period preference becomes stable after a short interval of responding, and can be reliably measured by a ratio on the subject's fourth minute of performance on the task. [p. 66]

This assumption of response stability, accepted without the use of nonreinforced control groups, is rendered ambiguous by the statistical artifact of regression to the mean.

The effect of regression to the mean occurs when later measures are performed on groups of subjects originally selected on the basis of their extreme scores. In regard to the preference-change score, the regression effect could stem from the selection of the subject's less-preferred response as the one to be reinforced. Using similar tasks and design, both Patterson and Hinsey (1964) and Cairns (1963) have demonstrated that regression to the mean, not differential reinforcement, provides a rather complete explanation of preference-change scores. In this regard, it is interesting to note that, where regression artifacts have been controlled by randomly selecting the response alternative to be reinforced, no significant difference between reinforcement and control groups was found (McCullers & Stevenson, 1960).

Another index of reinforcer effectiveness is rate of response, usually expressed as a difference score derived by subtracting the response rate during a base period from the response rate during an experimental period. Here, the questionable assumption is made that, in the absence of reinforcement, the response rates of children are stable over time. This assumption had led to studies lacking nonreinforced control groups because each subject is thought to be his own control (e.g., Grossman, 1963; Stevenson, 1961; Stevenson, Keen & Knights, 1963; Steveson & Knights, 1962; Stevenson & Odom, 1962). As Parton and Ross (1965) state,

> It is unlikely, however, that measures based on brief base periods can serve as controls for time-related changes such as warm-up effects, fatigue effects, and the effects of subjects' varying hypotheses and motivational states. [p. 67]

The issue of the subjects' varying motivational states is crucial, in that its treatment is relevant to all measures of social-reinforcement effectiveness. The assumption of a passive, receptive subject seems predicated on the ubiquitous definitions of reinforcement and nonreinforcement conditions used throughout these investigations. Certainly, there exists wide intersubject variability regarding a history with the stimulus events prescribed as "reinforcing" and "nonreinforcing" (Baron, 1966). Thus, as Bijou and Baer (1963) have indicated, the same stimulus may operate as a positive reinforcer for one child, a neutral event for another, and possibly even a punisher for a third. Similarly, it is uncertain that the events "good," "fine," and so on, naturally occur in adult–child interaction in any contingent, informationally relevant relationship (Paris & Cairns, 1972).

In addition to those methodological ambiguities just outlined, Parton and Ross (1965) also question what appears to be an unsystematic and potentially confounding selection of particular schedules of reinforcement delivery. For example, when interval schedules are used in conjunction with a rate-of-response index of reinforcement effect, it is impossible for the subject to change the number of reinforcements per unit time (e.g., Hartup, 1964; Stevenson, 1961; Stevenson & Fahel, 1961; Stevenson & Knights, 1962). Thus, the schedule in effect is "non-rate-contingent." Such a contingency likely would result in the development of response strategies unrelated to the empirical dependent variable.

Finally, Parton and Ross (1965) do not deny that the operant methodology has proven itself to be of value in the study of reinforcement effects with children. However, they note that "studies here reviewed abbreviated operant techniques by using only one estimation of baseline performance and one estimation of reinforced performance" (p. 71). Considering the pervasive problems of task appropriateness, experimental design, and statistical measurement evident with this line of research, it is difficult to agree with Eisenberger (1970) that "the evidence supports the view that deprivation–satiation operations change approval-contingent performance by altering the motivation for obtaining approval" (p. 273).

It should be noted that Zigler and his associates (e.g., Berkowitz Butterfield, & Zigler, 1965; Butterfield & Zigler, 1965; Zigler, 1963; Zigler & Kanzer, 1962) have modified the marble-in-the-hole (MITH) task such that many of the methodological issues raised by Parton and Ross (1965, 1967) are not problematic. The use of nonreinforced control groups, randomization of the response to be reinforced, and a persistence measure of reinforcer effectiveness produced less ambiguous results. Additionally, Zigler has investigated a number of subject and experimenter variables (e.g., age, sex, social class, locus of control, institutionalization) that affect the efficacy of reinforcement procedures. Although differing methodologically from the social drive–social reinforcement investigations discussed thus far, the efforts of Zigler and his co-workers are conceptually quite similar to the Gewirtz and Baer studies. On an a priori basis, both perspectives posit a monadic-reinforcement process as a central mechanism of social behavior, and both perspectives invoke intervening variables (deprivation–satiation states, valence hypothesis) to explain the operation of adults' verbal comments on children's motor behavior.

The Gewirtz and Baer interpretation of social reinforcer effectiveness has led to considerable debate among social-learning investigators, and a number of alternative explanations have been offered. For example, Walters and his colleagues (Walters & Karal, 1960; Walters & Ray, 1960; Walters, Marshall, & Shooter, 1960; Walters & Parke, 1964) have suggested that the difference between the isolated and nonisolated subjects in the original Gewirtz and Baer studies could be the result of the emotionally arousing nature of the isolation procedure, thereby rendering unnecessary the postulation of a social drive. A variety of other interpretations of the original Gewirtz and Baer data is available. These include a frustration hypothesis (Hartup & Himeno, 1959), and anxiety hypothesis (Stevenson & Hill, 1963), and an information hypothesis (Cairns, 1963). Stevenson (1965) has provided a particularly thorough treatment of these different positions, and it is clear from his review that no one theoretical framework can adequately account for the diverse effects of social reinforcement. What is unclear from the Stevenson review, however, are the theoretical and conceptual commonalities of these positions, and that of Gewirtz and Baer, which have shaped the prevailing learning-theory accounts of social behavior and socialization.

Initially, the empirical data offered in support of the various interpretations of the Gewirtz and Baer findings are largely predicated on the measurement of nonsocial motor behaviors. The units of behavior employed by these investigators, which include such discrete operants as manipulation of dolls, marbles, and other common objects, focus the attention of the experimenter *away* from any social interactive behavior on the part of the child. Also, each theoretical position prescribes a passive role for the child (subject), in which experimental contingencis come and go, each presentation operating with equal stimulus value. (This equality is assumed, not empirically verified.) Perhaps the multiple functions of stimulus events as described for different individuals (Bijou & Baer, 1963) are operable for the same individual within experimental sessions as well. Finally, these explanations of the Gewirtz–Baer data have invoked internal operations or intervening variables to explain the increased responsiveness of the subjects to the response-contingent stimuli. These drive states, frustration, and anxiety notions are of questionable utility in a theory of social behavior for two main reasons. For one, they are sufficiently broad and ambiguous to counteract any economy derived from subsuming observed relationships under the single proposition "frustration," or anxiety." And second, there seems to be no virtue in a descriptive statement that a child is "frustrated" or "anxious" unless other variables are added that will, together with internal, personal properties, specify what kind of behavior can be expected from him under some specific circumstances.

The Gewirtz–Baer hypothesis and the alternative interpretations of social reinforcer effectiveness promoted a state-of-the-organism orientation to social behavior. "State" is used here in accordance with Mischel's (1968) description in which he differentiated trait, state, and behavioral change variables as to their place of residence: intra- or extrapsychic. Thus, trait and state variables are similar, for his purposes, because both are intrapsychic. Behavioral change variables are differentiated from both trait and state variables because they are extrapsychic, or environmental.

The difference between trait, state, and behavioral change variables can be made clearer by specifying the types of causality each assumes. Dewey and Bentley's (1949) distinction between self-actional, interactional, and transactional causality appears relevant to this task. Trait variables appear to depend on a self-actional theory of causality. By "self-actional causality" it is meant that the cause of an event is seen as the event itself. Illness caused by demons within the body, landslides caused by the will of God, and low rates of social interaction caused by introversion all are examples of self-actional causality. In each case, there is no way to separate the event from its cause, because the event is also at least a part of the defining characteristics of the cause. As Mischel's (1968) review of the literature demonstrates, trait variables have very low predictive power for future behaviors. A like criticism is also appropriate for state-variable orientations.

State variables depend on an interactional theory of causality. By "interactional causality" it is meant that the cause of an event is seen as a result of the interaction of two or more factors, at least one of which is based on external events. For example, an individual possessing a high internal locus of control score will not display behaviors representative of his internal states in every situation. In other words, behavior in a given circumstance will, in part, be controlled by the unique features of the setting. In reference to the current theoretical explanation, a child's drive state for social reinforcers may be manipulated by varying the degree of availability of the reinforcer across time. Besides preserving a partly intrapsychic explanation of social behavior, the focus on drive-for-approval comments assumes an invariant, "reinforcing" quality to such utterances within experimental and naturalistic settings. However, there is growing body of laboratory research that indicates that positive social-reinforcement events are minimally effective in producing behavior change (e.g., Cairns, 1967; Curry, 1960; Spence, 1966). Also, information relevant to the circumstances under which social-reinforcement events typically occur in naturalistic settings indicate that these events do *not* occur in precise contingency relationships (Paris & Cairns, 1972).

Among the various interpretations of social-reinforcer effectiveness, the Gewirtz–Baer position has been dominant in the literature. As an explanatory theory of social behavior, the operant position suffers from a reliance on a limited view of behavior causation established on the basis of, and mainly supported by, nondevelopmental, unidirectional studies of animal and human learning.

The weakness of this learning-theory approach is nowhere more clearly revealed than in its treatment of the acquisition of a developmental sequence of behavior, or the acquisition of novel responses. Most accounts of the acquisition of novel responses frequently have been limited to descriptions of behavioral change based on principles of operant or instumental conditioning (Bijou & Baer, 1963; Lundin, 1961; Skinner, 1953). Skinner (1953) proposed a detailed account of the procedures of operant conditioning through successive approximations, whereby new patterns of behavior may be aquired. The validity of these processes for restricted learning settings is not questioned. However, the fact that many behavior topographies subsumed under the general rubric "social behavior," including cooperative play (Kirby & Toler, 1970), smiling (Brackbill, 1958), and vocalizations (Rheingold, Gewirtz, & Ross, 1959) have been brought under operant control in manipulative settings, gives no indication of the "natural" development and function of these behaviors in the child's interactions with adults and peer (Epstein, 1964). The issue at hand is methodological inadequacy, not illogical or ambiguious experimental analogies created by the laboratory investigator. Nor is the issue one of setting complexity. Rather, what seems critical in the measurement and analysis of social behavior is the restricted sampling by social drive–social reinforcement investigators of monadic, nonsocial behavior. It seems reasonable at this point to conclude that the discrete, singular unit of behavior and unit of analysis as used within the operant framework must be expanded in order to legitimately extend principles of learning to the study of the acquisition, maintenance, and modification of human behavior in dyadic and group situations. Lindsley's (1966) comments on the experimental analysis of social behavior are particularly insightful.

> Social emergents—social connotation, differential leadership, and human stimuli require special methods and treatment. The degree and direction of action of these social emergents could not have been accurately predicted by studying individuals in isolation. [p. 500]

However, in reviewing the current operant literature on social behavior as exemplified by the research contained in the *Journal of Applied Behavior Analysis* (e.g., Buell, Stoddard, Harris, & Baer, 1968; Hart, Reynolds, Baer, Brawley, & Harris, 1968; Kirby & Toler, 1970; O'Connor, 1969) and the *Journal of the Experimental Analysis of Behavior* (e.g., Schmitt & Marwell, 1968, 1971) the prevailing methodology is monadic in nature, with single responses of individuals serving as the principle unit of analysis (see Strain and Timm, 1974).

As Hartup (1970) suggests, it would be foolhardy to dismiss the contributions of operant research to the study of children's social behavior. The laboratory studies of social reinforcer effectiveness and the current applied literature on the effects of adult contingencies on child behavior have clearly demonstrated that direct, specified reinforcement from adults and peers can operate as a potent form of social influence. What is needed at this point, however, is an expanded, dyadic orientation to social behavior (e.g., Sears, 1951; Cairns, 1972).

BANDURA AND WALTERS SOCIAL-LEARNING CONCEPTS

The monadic, unidirectional features of the Gewirtz–Baer research are also present in the social-learning investigations of

Bandura and Walters (1963). Although many of their conceptualizations share with Gewirtz and Baer a common origin in the work of
Skinner (1938, 1953), their *theoretical statements* represent a distinct departure from the single-organism, single-response psychology of their contemporaries.

Bandura and Walters (1963) criticize other learning-theory approaches to social behavior for ignoring the measurement and
analysis of interactive behaviors. In turn, they propose a modification of various learning principles to naturalistic settings and the
formulation of new behavioral processess necessary to explain the
complexities of social behavior. Toward this end, their chief
contribution has been an extensive research effort to uncover the
role of imitation and vicarious reinforcement in the acquisition of
social behaviors.

Although social reinforcement is recognized as an important
means of shaping social behavior, Bandura and Walters contend
that many social responses are learned merely through observing
the behavior of other persons. As Parke (1969) notes, imitation
often "short-circuits" the shaping procedures involved in the use
of social reinforcement, and is, thus, one of the most important
means through which social responses are acquired and maintained.

A number of attempts have been made to account for the way in
which imitative responses are acquired; these have been reviewed
recently by Bandura (1965, 1969). Around the turn of the century,
social psychologists like Morgan (1896) and McDougall (1908)
offered explanations of imitation; however, like most instinct-
based theories, their explanations have not had much influence
(Parke, 1969).

More influential was a classical conditioning account of imitation
advocated by Humphrey (1921), Allport (1924), and Holt (1931).
According to this approach, person A makes a response that is
copied by person B. Then A may repeat the response, and a
circular associative sequence is set into action whereby B's matching behavior becomes a stimulus for A's behavior. Critics of the
theory (e.g., Bandura, 1965; Bandura & Walters, 1963) note that it
fails to account adequately for the emergence of novel responses
during the model–observer interaction sequence.

The instrumental learning paradigm has been used most frequently to explain the development of imitation. Miller and Dollard

provided the classic statement of this position over a quarter of a century ago in *Social learning and imitation* (1941). The authors describe a form of imitation called "matched-dependent" behavior. In a two-choice discrimination situation, children always saw the choice made by another subject rewarded. Whenever the observer matched the choice of the model, he was reinforced; nonmatching resulted in nonreinforcement. After a few trials, children learned to use the behavior of the model as a discriminative cue and thereby gained reinforcement. In this way, Miller and Dollard argued that children, as well as rats, could be taught to imitate the behavior of another person. In a variety of studies, they showed that imitative responses acquired in this manner would generalize across situations, models, and motivational states. However, in addition to requiring that the responses imitated already exist in the observer's repertoire, the theory does not account for the occurrence of imitative behavior in which the observer does not perform the model's responses during the acquisition process and for which reinforcers are not delivered to the models or the observers. Moreover , it represents imitative learning as contingent on the observer performing a close approximation to the matching response before he can acquire it imitatively and, thus, places a severe restriction on the behavioral changes that can be attributed to the influence of a model (Bandura & Walters, 1963).

Recently, evidence favoring an operant-reinforcement analysis of imitation has been presented by Baer and Sherman (1964). According to this position (Skinner, 1953), imitative responses develop from a learning history in which reinforcement is contingent on a response similar to the model's. As a result of being reinforced, the matching response itself may acquire secondary reinforcement properties. Through generalization, a child may eventually imitate responses of the model that have not been reinforced previously. In their research, Baer and Sherman (1964) employed an automated puppet that served as both the model and the reinforcing agent for shaping imitative behavior in children. They established a diverse repertoire of imitative responses (matching, head nodding, and novel verbalizations) by socially reinforcing the subjects for matching the responses of the puppet. Furthermore, these authors demonstrated that this imitative behavior will generalize to new behaviors (bar pressing in this (se) without specific training in the new response. Finally, their research indicates that the generalized imitative response can persist in a context of reinforcement of other imitative responses without being specifically reinforced.

In a later study, Baer, Peterson, and Sherman (1965) taught several imitative responses to retarded children whose behavior repertoire did not originally include imitation by physically assisting the child to make the desired responses initially and by providing immediate reinforcement for successful responses. The subjects were eventually capable of imitating new responses without assistance and showed evidence of generalized imitation as well.

Additionally, Lovaas, Berberich, Perloff, and Schaeffer (1966) successfully used a similar paradigm for conditioning imitation of verbal responses by mute schizophrenic children, and Metz (1965) showed that generalized imitative responding can be established by operant procedures in autistic children.

In order to account for the occurrence of imitative learning *outside* a reinforcement paradigm, Bandura (Bandura, 1965; Bandura & Walters, 1963) has offered a stimulus contiguity theory of observational learning. He has summarized this contiguity–mediational theory as follows:

> During the period of exposure, modeling stimuli elicit in observing subjects configurations and sequences of sensory experiences which, on the basis of past associations, become centrally integrated and structured into perceptual responses. [Bandura, 1965, p. 10]

According to Bandura, the observer's symbolic or representational responses in the form of images and verbal associates of the model's behavior are clearly central in accounting for observational learning. Bandura, Grusec, and Menlove (1966) report a test of this theory. On the assumption that the observer's verbalizations would affect the representational process, subjects were instructed to verbalize the model's actions in order to facilitate the development of symbolic representations of the model's responses. While other children "passively" observed, a third group verbalized competing or irrelevant responses in order to retard the acquisition of imaginal correlates of the model's behavior. In support of the theory, subjects in the facilitating symbolization condition were clearly superior in reproducing the model's responses. The study indicates that the nature of the activity (contextual arrangements) during the viewing period can markedly influence observational learning. More specifically, this research suggests that symbolization clearly enhances the acquisition of imitative responses. Finally, the study questions the adequacy of theories that stress the necessity of reinforcement for the occurrence of imitative learning.

Looking at the imitative paradigm as an explanatory construct, several conceptual and methodological problems, similar to those discussed for social drive–social reinforcement notions, are evident. The difficulties with imitation as an explanatory construct of social behavior begin with its inconsistent definition in the experimental literature. Of particular import here is the degree of match or sameness between the response components of the model and observer in determining the occurrence of a modeled response. Although the problem of response match has been alleviated in studies employing discrete operant measures of model and observer behavior (e.g., Baer & Sherman, 1964; Bandura & Kupers, 1964), investigators of aggressive, affiliative, and other significant social behaviors (e.g., Bandura, Ross & Ross, 1963; Marshall & Hahn, 1967) are unclear and inconsistent in specifying the necessary degree of match in imitative responding. Also, there is no consistent temporal limitation invoked between the termination of the model's response and the initiation of the observer's modeled behavior. Certainly, as this time interval becomes longer, any experimental control of confounding experiential variables is soon lost. Finally, the utility of "symbolic representation" as a primary mechanism of imitative learning is questionable until the precise observable concomitants of this process are specified.

Another major limitation of imitative learning (and social reinforcement) as an explanatory construct concerns the imposed unidirectional analysis of model–observer interaction. Bell (1968) has emphasized that such a perspective assumes a fixed and invariantly applied repertoire on the part of the model or actor, and a reciprocal and invariant passivity on the part of the observer or on the one acted upon. This review of imitation literature produced no investigation that proposes a role shift among model and observer, although repeated exchanges of model and observer functions are clearly evident in dyadic interactions, and are logically consistent with the explanatory status afforded imitative learning.

Finally, as a direct result of the definitional and conceptual limitations of imitative learning outlined earlier, there has been developed no methodology that can reliably assess the occurrence of model-observer behaviors in *ongoing* social interactions—a step necessary to determine the validity and generalizability of observational learning as an explanatory mechanism.

In summary, the operant and imitative-learning accounts of social behavior focus on unidirectional, singular, and often asocial events as their subject matter. Such an outcome seems inevitable given the monadic, unidirectional constructs that operant and imitative-learning theories have invoked.

Dyadic, Response-Support Conceptualizations

The major theoretical statement concerning the dyadic properties of social behavior was given by Sears (1951). In a historical review of social psychological research, Sears suggested,

> In spite of their long prepossession with social influences on the individual, psychologists think monadically. For them, the universe is composed of individuals. These individuals are acted upon by external events, to be sure, and in turn the external world is modified by the individual's behavior. But the universal laws sought by the psychologist almost always relate to a single body. They are monadic laws, and they are stated with reference to a monadic unit of behavior. [p. 478]

Central to the thesis of Sears' position is the distinction drawn between monadic and dyadic units of behavior. A schematic representation of a monadic action sequence is depicted in Figure 1.

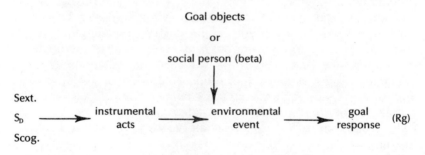

Figure 1   A monadic action sequence.

In Figure 1, the various potentialities for action are specified by S_D (motivation) and Scog (cognitive structure). The instrumental acts represent responses aimed at achieving a terminal goal (Rg). The most critical aspect of this scheme is the environmental event, as it is the necessary connecting link between a monadic and dyadic systematization of behavior. This concept refers to the changes produced in the environment by the instrumental activity; these are the changes necessary for the occurrence of the goal response. The child who is trying to engage a playmate in a cooperative building activity, for example, gets his reward when his associate begins passing him building materials. He therefore achieves the goal response, that is, plays cooperatively, when the environment changes, that is, when his playmate alters his behavior toward him. This unidirectional paradigm precisely fits the social reinforcement and imitation conceptualizations discussed earlier.

In contrast to the monadic unit just outlined, the dyadic unit is one that describes the combined action of two or more persons. The framework for such a description is shown in Figure 2.

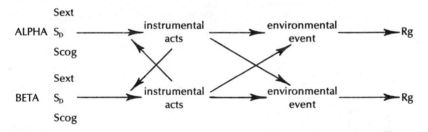

Figure 2   The dyadic sequence.

According to Sears (1951), a dyadic situation exists whenever two persons (Alpha and Beta) produce the environmental events for each other's goal response. The drives of each are thus satisfied only when the motivated actions of the other are carried through to completion. For example, the nurturant mother is satisfied by the cooing and smiling response of her infant when she comes into the child's view, and the child is satisfied by the presence of a familiar stimulus.

According to Sears (1951), the factor responsible for maintaining stability of the dyadic unit is the *expectancy* of the environmental event, diagrammed in Figure 3.

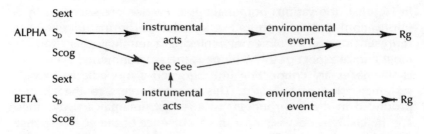

Figure 3   The dyadic sequence with anticipatory responses to the environmental event.

Sears explains the operation of the anticipatory responses as follows: "In the present case, the anticipatory response is a fractional part of the reactions Alpha makes to those behaviors of Beta that constitute the environmental event" (p. 480). For example, if a child wishes to build a tower with a peer, his partner must extend his hand to pass him a building part. He, in turn, must extend his hand to receive the object. These latter movements are the ones that fractionate and become anticipatory in Alpha's behavior sequence. And, as in the case of the anticipatory goal response, they elicit response-produced stimuli (Ree See) that become integrated into the total stimulus constellation that serves to instigate the behavior sequence on future occassions.

As Sears' (1951) notion of dyadic behavior sequences has been elaborated and given a sound empirical base (e.g., Bell, 1968, 1971, 1974; Cairns, 1972; Strain, 1974), its explanatory status as a mechanism for the acquisition and maintenance of social-interactive behaviors has been greatly enhanced. A most significant outcome of these empirical applications of Sears' theory has been the emergence of the notion that both members of a dyadic unit may alternately serve as elicitors and controllers of ongoing interactions. This *multidirectional* paradigm of analyzing interactions stands in sharp contrast to the unidirectional influence of social reinforcers or modeling stimuli advocated by the operant and social-learning theories discussed earlier.

RESPONSE-SUPPORT THEORY

Cairns' (1972) synthesis of the dyadic response components of attachment and dependency behaviors provides a particularly cogent and complete explication of this multidirectional paradigm. Cairns enumerates two major factors that contribute to the initial establishment of dyadic behaviors (within mother–infant interactions): (a) biogenic factors and (b) associational factors.

According to Cairns (1972), the appropriate place to begin a biogenic analysis of social-behavior development is at birth. In a review of infrahuman laboratory research, Cairns documents the emergence of dyadic, response-dependent sequences of behavior related to nursing, washing, grooming, and thermal regulation in mother–infant pairs.

The picture that emerges from this analysis of postpartum interactions is one in which biogenic variables stimulate the rapid evolution of a behavioral interdependence between the mother and her offspring. As Cairns (1972) concludes,

> The interaction chains that occur do not represent a smooth flow of events, but rather one in which the behaviors of the offspring (and the mother) serve to elicit a reciprocal response (environmental event in Sears' theory) in the other. As the interactions recur, the sequences themselves become more predictable and the behavioral episodes more regular. [p. 40].

Associational factors, which represent the second principle source for establishing dyadic behaviors, emphasize the operation of experience and learing. In effect, learning operates to regularize and bring interagent predictability to biogenically stimulated dyadic sequences. This process is analogous to the development of response expectancies described by Sears (1951). In the feeding sequence, for example, the responses of the mother may acquire significant cue properties for the elicitation, maintenance, and inhibition of the suckling responses of the infant. Likewise, the mother begins to discriminate and respond to nuances in the behavior of her offspring.

Both human and nonhuman infant studies of the conditioning process lend support to these associational processes. Several investigators (e.g., Lipsitt, 1967; Satinoff & Stanley, 1963; Thoman, Wetzel, & Levine, 1968) have demonstrated that events preparatory to and during the feeding sequence acquire elicitory and behavior-control properties. According to Cairns (1972), these cue properties serve to elicit and organize the behavior, as well as provide signals for its termination.

Cairns (1972) also indicates that response synchrony (dyadic behavior) does not account fully for the multiple ways by which social events can control the behavior of others. Social as well as nonsocial events have been shown to support dyadic behavior patterns in which they are not directly involved as manipulanda (Cairns, 1966; Walters & Parke, 1965). Again looking at the feeding sequence, the response of drinking is conditioned not only to the internal state (hunger cues) and the manipulanda (nipple or cup) but to the setting in which the feeding typically occurs. "The idea that the context plays a critical role in behavior support is not a new one, although it has rarely been invoked in discussion of social behavior" (Cairns, 1972, p. 42). This omission in particularly puzzling when one considers the setting and context-specific quality of social behaviors (e.g., fighting, affectional responses) throughout ontogeny.

A critical component in Cairns' (1972) analysis of dyadic patterns of behavior is the proposed "behavioral maintenance" or "response-support" functions of social events. Those events, which Cairns designates as possessing response-support properties, have typically been classified as having reinforcing potential. To clarify the distinction between reinforcing and response-support qualities of social events, it is necessary to determine the possible functions of "reinforcing" or "response-support" occurrences. For instance, events that can elicit and maintain sucking (e.g., pacifier, nipple, thumb) tend to become preferred objects. If they are presented to the organism during periods of arousal or anxiety, they also have the capacity to inhibit distress and reorganize behavior patterns. As Cairns (1972) notes, the usual system for conceptualizing these events has been to assign them reinforcement status. Although this "explanation" preserves the reinforcment account of social interaction, its irreconcilable demand for a posteriori classification of events as reinforcers or nonreinforcers makes these very notions virtually impossible to disprove.

With interactional sequences of behavior as the scientific subject matter, the classification of events as "reinforcing" is made more dubious by the necessity of arbitrarily assigning temporal parameters to the operation of reinforcing events. Examples of the problems inherent in this assignment task are reported by Kopfstein (1972) and by Patterson and Cobb (1970). In both investigations, an attempt was made to demonstrate, by naturalistic methods, the operation of various social events (consequences) that were predicted to accelerate to decelerate rates of aggressive behavior. In a population of mentally retarded preschoolers, Kopfstein (1972), found *no* evidence that "positive" social consequences accelerated aggressive behavior, or that "negative" social consequences had an inhibitory effect on assaultive behaviors. Similar findings were reported by Patterson and Cobb (1970) with a group of adolescent boys observed in their homes. Each observational system provided coded classifications of two-step behavior sequences (e.g., Subject response A – Peer consequence A) into time intervals, and both investigators hypothesized the effects of consequent events to be operable within the time interval immediately following their occurrence. The general disconfirmatory nature of their findings makes the assignment of an "effective" temporal period for reinforcing events highly suspect. In their concluding analysis of the reinforcement control of sequential interactions, Patterson and Cobb offer the view that the behaviors composing sequences of interactions are more directly a function of stimulus or eliciting events rather than accelerating or decelerating consequences. This proposal seems quite consistent with Cairns' (1972) notion that social events provide the setting or set the occasion for interdependent behavior.

BELL'S SOCIALIZATION MODEL

In his classic analysis of the "direction of effects" in studies of socialization, Bell (1968, 1971, 1974) proposes a similar stimulus or response-support dimension to social events. A description of Bell's (1968) conceptualization of the socialization process and the research from which he draws support seems appropriate here, as it demonstrates the broad, integrative power of dyadic analysis as an explanatory mechanism of social behavior.

Bell (1968) notes that most research on parent–child interaction has been directed to the unidirectional question of effects of parents on children (e.g., Hawkins, Peterson, Schweid, & Bijou, 1966; Wahler, Winkel, Peterson, & Morrison, 1965). Such an emphasis seems entirely consistent with, and most likely a result of, the general monadic thrust of experimental psychology. Prior to Bell's paper, only one major work on the socialization of the child acknowledged that "the model of a unidirectional effect from parent to child is overdrawn, a fiction of convenience rather than belief" (Sears, Maccoby, & Levin, 1957, p. 141). It is an oddity that many of the learning theory models of socialization took for granted the general likelihood of finding antecedent or consequent control over child behavior but not over parental behavior as well. The choice would seem to have been based on philosophical–historical tradition, not empirical evidence.

Bell (1968) has assembled a compelling array of human and infrahuman data discordant with the parent-effect model. For instance, at the human level, Rheingold (1966) has pointed to the disproportionate amount of attention afforded to infants who become a part of some human group. The appearance of the most homely of infants is unquestionably a powerful stimulus for a wide variety of adult affectional behaviors (e.g., gazing at infant, smiling at infant, playfully touching infant). Likewise, infant crying can be observed to elicit a multitude of sometimes effective adult coping behaviors. Studies of variations in parental behavior with different children provide another piece of data discordant with the parent-effect model (e.g., Lasko, 1954; Schaefer, 1963; Stott, 1941; Yarrow, 1963). Additionally , the ability of the child (infant) to set the tone or intensity of interaction is well-documented in studies of infant state (e.g., Levy, 1958; Stern, 1974). Briefly, these results indicate that, as infants exhibit various states of arousal or wakefulness during the feeding–sleeping cycle, they elicit caretaker behaviors compatible with their degree of arousal.

Research on lower animals provides even stronger evidence of the stimulating and selective effect of offspring on their caretaker's behavior (Bell, 1968). Rheingold (1963) has compiled an extensive report on the influence of the young on maternal behavior from the deer mouse to the baboon. An example is the incidence in which the clinging "infant" behaviors of newborn rhesus monkeys fostered with nonlactating females induced maternal responsiveness and biochemically normal lactation (pp. 268–299). In a similar though expanded study, Beach and Jaynes (1956) manipulated the appearance and behavior of offspring so as to identify specific classes of stimuli that control parent behavior. Visual, olfactory, tactile, thermal, and movement cues from rat pups were shown to be capable of inducing maternal retrieval, being effective individually and in combination. Bell (1968) highlights two implications of this research on animal behavior. If variations in offspring behavior can so radically modify what are considered to be rigid behavior patterns of animal parents, even greater effects would be expected on human parental behavior, which is presumably more plastic and susceptible to all classes of influence. The second point concerns the variety of offspring stimulus parameters demonstrated to control parental behavior. It should not be unreasonable to accept a multidirectional-effect model if one grants that offspring are at least sources of stimuli.

Taken together, the theoretical and empirical efforts of Sears (1951), Bell (1968, 1971, 1974), and Cairns (1972) provide an integrative and coherent system for conceptualizing interactive behavior. At least four major commonalities are evident in each work, which provide a salient contrast to the social drive–social reinforcement conceptualizations of social behavior described in the preceding section.

First, these response-support notions take sequential social interactions as their scientific subject matter. In doing so, they focus primarily on in vivo observations rather than on experimental, manipulative tactics of research. As Cairns (1972) notes, such an orientation leads to an approach to social behaviors as context-sensitive events. Second, the occurrence of individual responses from each member of the interacting dyad has an equal potential for instigating, maintaining, or terminating the interaction sequence. This open-ended approach to the classification and prediction of behavioral events is a method of significant influence in ethology and zoology; and recently it has been successfully applied to the behavioral study of autistic children (Hutt & Vaizey, 1966), and preschoolers' interactive behavior (Blurton Jones, 1972; McGrew, 1972; Ray, 1974). An additional commonality among these positions is the emphasis upon the ontogenetic quality of interdependent behavior. This developmental focus has been put succinctly by Cairns (1972). Organismic and associational factors are proposed to interact in controlling the direction and course of dyadic behavior through ontogeny. According to Cairns,

> An examination of the young animal's behavior as he progresses from infancy through adolescence to early adulthood indicates that some of the more important changes in dyadic interactions are linked to alterations in his bio-physical state. [p. 43]

This description is complicated by the fact that modifications in biophysical state can be either a determinant or an outcome of changes in dyadic interaction patterns. Thus, the interaction sequences between two organisms are dynamic and continuously vulnerable to external or internal stimulus changes. Finally, these positions are linked together in their concern for determining the *function* of social behaviors to the organism. This has been described in terms of achieving mutual goal responses (Sears, 1951), setting the occasion for and organizing behavior (Cairns, 1972), and activating and selecting reciprocal hierarchies of behavior (Bell, 1968).

In summarizing the two principal theoretical systems of social behavior discussed thus far, several points are of critical importance. Initially, there can be no question as to the guiding force that theoretical assumptions of social behavior have played in determining the "appropriate" topographic and contextual parameters for social-behavior research. Contrast, for example, the singular response units advocated by operant psychologists (e.g., Gewirtz & Baer, 1958; Hart *et al.*, 1968) with the dyadic response sequence supported by Cairns (1972). In addition, a theoretical shift is evident in the literature which in part locates the "motivation" for social behavior in the stimulus dimensions of the *other's* behavior, not as an intrapsychic phenomenon. As a result, the dyadic position has generated research aimed specifically at determining the stimulus effects of one person's behavior on that of his associate's, and vice versa.

Ethological Theory of Social Behavior

The application of ethological methods and theory to human social behavior is in its infancy. Nevertheless, the publication of recent works on the ethological analysis of children's social behavior by Blurton Jones (1972), Hutt and Hutt (1970), McGrew (1972), and Ray (1974) are impressive in their detail and potential contribution to the ontogenetic study of the child.

The dominant viewpoint in ethology regarding the utility of theoretical postulates and theorems has at best been skeptical. Lehrman (1953), Hinde (1959), and Blurton Jones (1972) have proposed that theories have more often concealed ignorance than explained facts. Thus, when one speaks of an ethological "theory" of social behavior, some clarification is warranted. Ethological "theory" may be restated in terms of several generally accepted suppostions regarding social behavior and its most complete measurement.

First, social behaviors are considered to be reducible to a large variety of simple observable features of behavior. The features have typically taken the form of gestures, body postures, and visual fixations, or *actones* in Wright's (1960) system of unitizing behavioral elements. The reduction of the behavioral stream by ethologists to molecular features of behavior is distinguished from an analogous technique in operant psychology on the basis of *response variability*. Whereas slight modifications in response topography are carefully recorded by ethologists as meaningful events, with potential discriminative properties, the operant psychologist is concerned with grouping topographically distinctive behaviors in terms of their common, and experimentally controlled, environmental effect.

According to Hutt and Hutt (1970), gestures, postures, and visual fixations are the essential raw material of behavior. These elements have been shown to play subtle and vital roles in social interaction, their distribution in time providing basic information about the effects of the environment upon behavior and underlying functions of the behavior (e.g., Brannigan & Humphries, 1972; Scheflen, 1963). For example, Brannigan and Humphries (1972) have provided a "tentative" list of some 136 nonverbal signals used by preschool children in social interaction. Of these signals, 40 consist of muscular changes in the mouth region, each of which provides the child's partner with discriminative cues for subsequent behavior! Such a finding poses some very serious conceptual and methodological problems for the current usage and measurement of "smile" as a dependent variable, or as a social reinforcer in psychological research.

Additionally, the use of observable motor behaviors allows for more explicit data collection and treatment procedures than are available in studies using rating scales or large predetermined categories of behavior. For example, a particular facial posture may be measured according to its frequency, mean duration, total time spent in relation to other behaviors, and the latency between its occurrence and the onset of another organism's responses. Furthermore, any statistical manipulations that meet the necessary scaling and sampling assumptions may be applied to the resulting data.

A second major ethological supposition regarding social behavior concerns the influence of conspecifics' behavior. The social responses of the organism are seen as being inextricably tied to the actor's own physiological condition as well as to the behavior of others in some antecedent–consequent relationship. Whereas some patterns of behavior may be regarded as endogenously motivated, others clearly are initiated by responses of other organisms. Thus, it is necessary to record the behaviors of both animals in the temporal order in which they occur. Each motor pattern of one animal may then be treated as either stimulus or response to the adjacent responses of the other. On this ground, the measurement techniques of ethology are indistinguishable from the dyadic response analysis of Sears (1951) and Cairns (1972). The emphasis on dyadic analysis has produced a number of sophisticated observational and statistical methods for analyzing sequential behaviors (see Altmann, 1965; Grant, 1963; Strain, 1974). The recording and analysis of sequential social events assume that elements of behavior are not juxtaposed randomly; some behaviors occur more frequently in temporal juxtaposition with each other than with others. Thus, on the basis of recording a few specific motor patterns, ethologists have been able to predict the outcome of a particular action sequence (Hutt & Hutt, 1970). Typically, such judgments have been made by calculating the statistical dependency between events. Altmann (1965), Bobbitt, Jensen, and Kuehn (1964), and Raush (1965) have provided detailed discussions of attempts to apply interaction analysis to social behavior. Additionally, Hutt and Hutt (1970), have outlined the potentials of chi-square, factor analytic, and informational models for determining interdependencies among sequential events.

Another ethological supposition regarding social behavior concerns the biological or survival function of social acts. According to Blurton Jones (1972), the concept of "man as animal" is at the heart of the ethological method of studying human behavior. In the past, the ethological emphasis on the survival value of social behaviors was seen as requiring a catalogue of ubiquitous biological drive states, the dynamics of which were determined by behaviors directed to or in response to conspecifics. More recently, however, ethologists have abandoned the search for physiological and psychological correlates of drive conditions, and studied the survival value or function of social behaviors in reference to salient environmental circumstances (e.g., Hutt & Ounsted, 1966; Hutt & Vaizey, 1966; McGrew, 1972). For example, Hutt and Ounsted (1966) have provided an extensive film record of eight autistic children who exhibited gaze aversion from the face of peers and adults. When analyzed in sequential fashion in relation to the behaviors of proximate adults and children, gaze aversion was demonstrated to occur within an alternating-response cycle of "visual regard–gaze avert–visual regard–gaze avert," and so on. Since the initiation and termination of the individual response components of this sequence were shown to be temporally related to proximity and head orientation of conspecifics, the gaze averting behavior was likely functioning as a regulatory mechanism, periodically adjusting sensory input. More recently, Hutt and Hutt (1970) have suggested that longer and more frequent eye contacts with autistics are possible given the establishement of dyadic or synchronous response patterns between the autistic child and his partner. Note that this process is quite similar to Cairns' (1972) notions regarding the development and regularization of dyadic-response patterns between mother–infant pairs. Hutt and Ounsted's functional-dyadic analysis of gaze aversion stands in sharp contrast to the typical intrapsychic interpretations given this behavior (e.g., Creak, 1961). As Mischel (1968) notes, intrapsychic interpretations provide little more than a nominal classification of behavior events. Additionally, it is unlikely that an operant analysis of gaze aversion would uncover a predictable reinforcing event for this response.

In summary, the ethological approach to social behavior supports a dyadic analysis of interactive events. In so doing, ethologists have recorded the sequential behaviors of dyad members as their primary subject matter. Although the ethological method yields descriptive rather than analytic information, it represents the necessary beginning point for the scientific study of social behavior.

Direct Observational Systems

It is important to note at the outset of this section that a comprehensive review of direct observational systems concerned with measuring interactive behavior is beyond the scope and intent of this volume. Rather, illustrative examples of three major methodologies (diary record, time and event sampling, ethological system) will be provided in order to construct an historical review of the field, and to highlight the influence of the previously discussed theories on these observational systems.

Hutt and Hutt (1970) have commented that the problems of accurately recording social interactions of several individuals greatly tax the behavioral scientist. Not only are social behaviors inherently subtle and complex, but the fact that in any natural social situation there are usually a number of individuals interacting and moving about maginfies the task of tracking a specific individual or reliably recording particular encounters. Attempts have been made to circumscribe the problems as much as possible by reducing the number in the group, by marking the individuals and following them individually, or by recording only certain preselected activities.

DIARY RECORDS

Under the impetus of the child-development research movement sponsored by the National Research Council during the years 1920–1935, numerous programs of observational research on preschool children's behavior were undertaken. The initial efforts to records the social contacts of preschool children employed diary record accounts. The method involves a sequential diary account of growth changes and behavior episodes from the life history of the child. Notations are made from day to day, and episodes that illustrate various behavioral processes are described narratively. Typically, these diary accounts were taken by a single observer who functioned primarily as a behavioral stenographer, writing longhand comments regarding the interactions of a particular child or group of children. Although these efforts are commendable in the sense of attempting to capture the complete contextual arrangements in which social interactions occur, the general interpretive, novelese character of the data provided only a gross topographic picture of the development and maintenance of child–child interactions.

Additionally, diary records, when analyzed for exact information as to the normal frequency of particular modes of behavior under given conditions, yielded data of doubtful reliability because of the inevitable incompleteness and inconsistency of the sampling of particular items and the slow and cumbersome nature of the recording process. These data were dubious also because the selection of events to be recorded was dependent upon the judgment of the individual observer and because the transcription of these events was in purely qualitative terms that varied for different observers and for the same observer at different times. As a medium for the accumulation of reliable information concerning the incidence and patterning of social behaviors, therefore, the diary record was distinctly unsatisfactory (Arrington, 1943; Barker, 1930).

Notwithstanding these rather pervasive criticisms regarding biased response selection, unreliable recording, inefficient gathering of data, and unwarranted observer interpretations, the basic method has unique advantages in principle. Initially, by using written records, it allows the transcription of subtle changes in behavior topography and context, not available in standardized checklists or rating-scale techniques. Secondly, the "open" character of the records gives a multidimensional picture of simultaneous and successive factors in the behavior and circumstances of an individual child (Wright, 1960). Finally, diary descriptions take into account the continuity of behavior as this can be done only by observations of children, one by one, over extended periods of time. In this regard, diary records, more than any other observational system, provide a longitudinal view of behavior development and differentiation.

During the period in which these records were specifically analyzed to study the development of interactive responses in preschool children, the dominant social-behavior theory of the day was Freudian, and the content of these records often contained psychoanalytic interpretations of child behavior. For example, a portion of the records cited by Wright (1960) reads as follows:

> One day when, after being rejected from a play group, he broke into a more than usually violent fit of crying. A playmate asked him why he was so upset; whereupon he replied, "Cause you treat me like a pig." This is significant because it shows the development of the conscious sense of self. [p. 452]

As is evident from this excerpt and the previous discussion of diary record methods, the influence of Freudian thought did not restrict the number, type, or complexity of behaviors recorded (as have other conceptualizations of social behavior); rather, it fostered an interpretive quality to the records, whereby the observer analyzed incidents in relation to psychosexual stages, ego conflicts, or system unconscious properties.

TIME AND EVENT SAMPLING

In contrast to the "open," interpretive quality of diary records, time and event sampling procedures represent "closed" observational systems in which the observer fixes his attention upon preselected aspects of behavior (Wright, 1960). The distinctions between time and event sampling principally concern the use of contextual cues and the complexity of the unit of behavior to be recorded. Whereas time-sampling procedures are aimed at recording the occurrence of specific behavior topographies as they occur, regardless of the context in which they occur, the event-sampling procedure is concerned with detailing the setting parameters and contextual arrangements in which a specified behavior occurs (e.g., Dawe, 1934). Similarly, a number of distinct response topographies would be subsumed under a specified behavior unit (e.g., "cooperative play" used by Parten, 1932) in the time-sampling procedure. On the other hand, an event sampling of "cooperative play" behavior would likely include a more precise accounting of the specific events categorized as "cooperative play."

Time and event sampling are, however, included together in this discussion for several reason. Both types of systems yield readily comparable data as a result of focusing upon a restricted number of behavioral phenomenon. Second, both methods have been greatly concerned with questions of reliability of measurement. In this regard, they can be seen as a *reaction* to diary accounts, not as an historical development of these anecdotal records. Finally, both methods reflect a similar line of influence from early experimental (laboratory) research to current operant suppositions of behavior. Time sampling has been by far the preferred method of child study and, as such, it will be given primary attention.

With a view to increasing the reliability and compatibility of behavior records, various controls were introduced into the study of social interaction. One most important change evidenced in time-sampling procedures was the translation of observed events into readily comparable quantitative terms through the use of time as a common denominator, and the systematic rotation of observations to reduce the effect of uncontrolled variables in the situation. The technique, which equated the number and length of observations for all individuals or groups to be studied, attempted to provide a legitimate base for the comparison of measures of behavior frequency.

Other controls (also present in event-sampling methods) designed to facilitate the recording process and to insure consistent recording of the same events by different observers, included the substitution of prepared record blanks and code symbols for longhand description, the limitation of the number of behavior items or categories to that which could be reliably recorded at one time by one person, and the definition of the behavior to be observed in precise objective terms (e.g., Beaver, 1932; Green, 1933; Parten, 1932). As Arrington (1943) comments,

> Contrasted with the experimental method, it (time sampling) is a form of controlled observation in which the observer, the method of recording, and the manner of selecting the behavior to be observed are subject to control rather than the situation in which observations are made. [p. 82]

In summary, the time-sampling method has provided a number of contributions to observational study. It permits systematic control by selection of phenomena to be observed and studied. It insures reliability and representativeness by recording large numbers of commensurable observations. It is economical in research time and effort. Its coding schemes minimize equivocal judgments and prescribe definite criteria to quantify whatever is observed. Finally, it goes far to achieve standardization of observer and behavior code as measuring instruments.

The influence of the prevailing experimental zeitgeist in psychology during the 1930s is quite evident from an examination of the early time-sampling of social-interaction studies. Parten's (1932) classic investigation of the play behavior of preschool children provides an illustrative example of this influence. In an effort to record each child's level of social participation during free play, Parten devised a six-unit scale of interaction, including (a) unoccupied behavior, (b) solitary play, (c) onlooker behavior, (d) parallel play, (e) associative play, and (f) cooperative or organized play. Each child was observed separately for 1 minute each day, 5 days per week, over 8 months.

In Parten's time-sampling method, several suppositions regarding the study of behavior in general, and social behavior in particular, are salient. In the development of the behavioral categories, many topographically dissimilar behaviors are grouped together to establish "discrete" units of activity (e.g., solitary play). This effort is in many ways similar to, and most likely a derivative of, a parallel development in laboratory research whereby experimental manipulanda were introduced to provide a discrete measure of animal behavior, that is, instrumental act. As Tinbergen (1951) noted, the use of discrete, singular units of behavior are entirely appropriate for an analytic science concerned with the "whys" of behavior. However, Tinbergen further comments that,

> in its haste to step into the twentieth century and to be a respectable science, psychology skipped the preliminary descriptive stage that other natural sciences had gone through, and so was soon losing touch with the natural phenomenon. [p. 87]

Secondly, although Parten's (1932) aim was to provide normative data on the *social* participation of the children she observed, the behavior-sampling system of 1-minute observation time on each child separately could produce only monadic, nonsocial information. No index is provided for determining the behavior of other children toward the target child, nor is the social context of the target child's behavior recorded.

Finally, the use of such a limited time-unit sample prohibits any determination of the sequential effects of one form of social participation or contact on another. Likewise, there is no way to determine the possible functional effects that one child's behavior might have on another's. Parten's work is by no means unique in its conception and design. Similar notions of observing and analyzing social behavior are present in studies of quarrels (Green, 1933; Jersild & Fite, 1937), social interaction (Arrington, 1932; Mallay, 1935), and competition (Bott, 1928; Updegraff & Herbst, 1933; Van Alstyne, 1932).

Whereas the essentially monadic, nonsocial methods of the early time-sampling studies were most likely a fortuitous outcome of a prevailing scientific attitude in psychology itself, the present-day use of time-sampling techniques to measure the social behavior of preschoolers is closely tied to operant conceptualizations of social behavior and its measurement. Currently, there exists a growing body of observational research regarding the operant properties of children's behavior in relation to adult mediated contingencies. These time-sampling studies have typically been concerned with ameliorating isolate behavior patterns in specific children by selectively providing adult attention for nonisolate or cooperative activity (e.g., Buell, Stoddard, Harris, & Bear, 1968; Hart et al., 1968). For example, in the study by Hart et al. (1968), the major behavior observed and treated experimentally was cooperation between an isolate child and her peers. Cooperative play was defined as any of the following activities:

> pulling a child or being pulled by a child in a wagon, handing an object to a child, or pouring into his hands or into a container held by him; helping a child by supporting him physically, or bringing, putting away, or building something verbalized as expressly for him; sharing something with a child by digging in the same hole, carrying the same object, painting on the same paper or from the same pot, or adding to the same structure or construction. [p. 74]

Additionally, the target child's proximity to other children was recorded. Proximity was defined as being within 3 feet of another child, indoors, and within 6 feet outdoors. The subject's behaviors were recorded in consecutive, 10-second intervals during the school-day session. The child's scores for any day were the percentage of 10-second intervals marked as involving proximity or cooperative play.

The similarities between this investigation and Parten's (1932) study are remarkable. First of all, one finds the use of categorical behavior items—that is, solitary play, cooperative play—that cover such a broad spectrum of child behavior that the resulting frequency or percentage of interval accounting of response occurrences is equivocal. Also, there is an absence of data in both studies on the behavior of the target child's peers. This fact is, of course, consistent with the monadic, unidirectional view of social behavior supported by the general social drive–social reinforcement literature. Finally, the 1-minute time interval used by Parten (1932) and the forced-frequency time intervals employed by Hart *et al.* (1968) prohibit any sequential analysis of child–child interactions, and thus leave unanswered the question of what effects one individual's behavior has on another's, and vice versa.

The limitations that these and other investigators have placed upon the unit of behavior in naturalistic social-interaction research can be viewed in part as reflecting an avid concern with the reliability of their measures. As the case was put by Gellert (1955), "the fewer the categories of behavior, the greater will be the reliability of the data" (p. 194). And it would appear that a devotion to reliability has been preeminent among many investigators of social interaction. It is ironic that the principle strength of time-sampling procedures, namely, the reliability of the records, has so restricted the subject matter of these investigations.

The whole issue of reliability is so complex and confused in the literature that it requires a separate, albeit brief, treatment. When discussing reliability, one would do well to paraphrase the Mad Hatter and specify that, "when I talk of reliability I mean what I say, and nothing more than what I say." For example, Medley and Mitzel (1963) and Patterson (1967) propose that reliablity includes observer agreement and stability across situations. Medley and Mitzel, however, also include the ability of the instrument to differentiate situations. Bijou, Peterson, and Ault (1968) pay attention solely to observer agreement.

In observational research, the only feasible test of reliability is interobserver agreement. In early observational studies, observer-agreement scores were obtained primarily by correlation coefficients. However, high interscorer correlations are difficult to interpret because it is possible for scorers to disagree on many items (temporally) and yet have equal total scores; and it is also possible for one scorer consistently to give higher scores than the other, a difference that could not be detected in the correlation coefficient. A more favored method of obtaining interobserver agreement would be a concordance measure between scorers, whereby percentage of agreement is made on the basis of an item-by-item or within-interval comparison of data points (e.g., Solomon & Wahler, 1973).

Even when a strict concordance measure is applied to observation data, the observer-agreement measure is not a wholly satisfactory criterion for the reason that it is a relative rather than an absolute measure which does not differentiate the good observer from the poor observer (Hutt & Hutt, 1970). In addition, recent evidence (Reid, 1970; Romanczyk, Kent, Diament, & O'Leary, 1973) indicates that reliability assessment is a *reactive* process, that obtained reliability coefficients do *not* reflect the general adequacy of the observational process at times when reliability is not being measured. Romanczyk et al. (1973) have demonstrated further that observers shift their observational criteria to match the idiosyncratic criteria employed by reliability assessors. It is only to be expected that, after sufficient training, two observers can come to share each other's interpretations. As far as communication with later readers is concerned, agreement with an untrained observer or observers well might be considered of greater interest. This would give an indication of how well the verbal category definitions can be understood by someone who does not have the benefit of the author's personal training in their interpretation.

In review, the time-sampling technique has been a frequently used research tool in psychology, Its exactness of behavioral classification, comparability of behavior frequencies, and standardization of observer functions serve to demonstrate the reliability of the method. However, as used and influenced by many investigators of social interaction, its utility is equivocal. The types of control that have fostered high interobserver agreements also bring the *validity* of this technique into serious question (Hutt & Hutt, 1970; Smith & Connolly, 1972; Wright, 1960). Validity, as discussed by Wright (1960), refers to the "naturalness" of the behavior observed and the adequacy with which it is sampled. As expressed in earlier sections of this book, the central conceptual and methodological issue in social-behavior research concerns the representativeness of the unit of behavior. It has been proposed that monadic, social-reinforcement conceptualizations of social behavior are inadequate; likewise, considering the monadic, unidirectional quality of much time-sampling data, it is unlikely that this method can be legitimately referred to as a valid index of dyadic, interactive behaviors.

To summarize in brief, some characteristics of the time-sampling *and* event-sampling literature on the social behavior of preschool children which limit its utility are:

1. A prevalent bias in the categories used and situations examined toward behavior of a monadic quality.
2. The use of a small number of highly complex categories, with resultant emphasis on high interobserver agreement after considerable training.
3. The lack of sequential analsysis of behavior occurrences, or temporal association of behavior clusters in specific situations.

These criticisms are not, of course, entirely inherent within time-sampling methods; rather, they reflect a dominant use by experimenters of global, monadic units of measurement.

ETHOLOGICAL METHOD

The method of child study that has been most concerned with the validity of its procedures has been the ethological approach. In so doing, this observational method corrects many of the weaknesses found in time-sampling measures. Similarly, it incorporates many of the conceptual notions of social behavior evident in the response-support and ethological theories of social behavior.

Several features of the ethological study of social behavior have been mentioned earlier. Briefly, the unit of behavior in ethological research is initially limited to gestures, postures, and visual fixations. These motor acts are then recorded and analyzed in a continuous fashion (usually by video tape) in order to obtain information regarding the sequencing or patterning of social interaction. Finally, behavioral records of different species types are frequently compared to find points of behavioral or situational correlation.

In addition to these features of ethological observation, this approach is distinctive in its usual length of observation or number of data points collected, its creation of second-order behavior categories (e.g., "rough and tumble play" as used by Blurton Jones, 1972), and its interexperiment strategy of reliability assessment.

The ethologists' concern with a detailed knowledge of the complete behavioral repertoire of their subjects has made ethological studies of children's social behavior a long and laborious task.

It would not be unusual for such a method to be used over a period of several months or years on a group of children (e.g., Blurton Jones, 1972; McGrew, 1972). Given the extensive descriptive treatment of behavioral phenomena by this method, it is not surprising that the approach is often compared to ecological research, the goal of which is "to describe the life situations of individuals "(Wright, 1967, p. 1). In practice, however, these systems have little in common. Whereas the ethologist is concerned with the patterning of discrete motor acts (e.g., smile, hit at) between individuals, the unit of measurement for ecological workers includes sequences of goal-directed behaviors, such as walking to school, playing catch, or getting out of bed. Of course, the goal-directedness of behavior is an internal state or motivation inferred by the observer. Such a judgment is antithetical to ethological methods. As Hutt and Hutt (1970) comment, the procedure is "well beyond the scope of scientific description" (p. 23).

In its concern for minimizing observer interpretations, the ethological approach is more closely aligned with the familiar baseline phase in behavior analysis research (see Dinsmoor, 1966; Gelfand & Hartmann, 1968). These systems differ, however, in that the descriptive phase of ethological investigations obtain considerably more data points on a larger spectrum of behavior. Additionally, measures of behavior topography, duration, rate, and latency are employed by ethologists, whereas the behavior-analytic research is predicated on the sensitivity of rate measures (e.g., Bijou, Peterson, Harris, Allen, & Johnston, 1969; Skinner, 1938). The point of argument here is more general than a concern over the exclusive use of rate of responding as the central measure of behavior. Recall, the operant assumption of a ubiquitous reinforcing (stimulus) event, is functionally related to an invariant, discrete operant (e.g., marble drop, lever press). It may be argued that it is of no possible relevance how the animal makes his response (operant) if consistent regularities in the shapes of cumulative frequency curves, with different responsive-reinforcement contingencies, obtain. That rate is not always a sensitive behavioral measure, however, is shown by two recent studies, one involving monkeys, the other, 3–5-year-old children.

In a study by Butler and Harlow (1954), it was reported that monkeys would persist in opening the door to their cage for periods exceeding 9 hours, with visual exploration of the labora-

tory as the only reward. Several years later, Symmes (1959) repeated this investigation, and obtained quite identical response
curves. In addition, Symmes made the following observations on
the monkeys' behavior after several hours of maintaining opening
and looking behavior:

> Subjects were not exploring visually during all the response time.
> They appeared to spend more than half the response time manipulat-
> ing the door, chewing on the sill, and exploring tactually what they
> could not see through the open door. [p. 186]

Taking the number of door openings as the sole measure of
behavior, it appears that investigative behavior was maintained at a
high level for hours on end. By taking cognizance of the kinds of
morphological changes that occurred, a rather different picture
emerges. It would appear that there was a gradual waning of
specific investigation of the laboratory which was replaced by more
generalized activities. A count of number of door openings is
misleading unless it is accompanied by detailed behavioral observations.

In a study of exploratory behavior in young children (Hutt &
Ounsted, 1966), a novel object was presented under different
conditions of auditory and visual feedback. Counters in the object
registered each manipulatory movement so that a reading of them
would give a measure of how much a child had responded to the
object. The results showed that exploration increased with successive exposures when auditory feedback was contingent on manipulation. What is more unique, however, is the reported change in
the topography of response directed toward the object. During the
first few exposures, the children primarily investigated the object.
After some trasitional phases of exploratory activity, investigation
ceased and, by the fifth or sixth exposure, play activities were the
most prominent responses. From these data, it would appear that
the addition of detailed observations of behavior in psychological
experiments may throw light directly on the behavioral mecha-
nisms activated by a particular set of environmental variables.

Another distinguishing characteristic of the ethological method
is the procedure by which ethologists have developed second-
order behavior categories (e.g., rough and tumble play, social
exchange of objects) from clusters of gestures, postures, and visual

fixations. In contrast to much psychological research, ethology concentrates on the derivation of behavior categories from data rather than from theory, convention, or previous research. For instance, is there any use in looking for causal controls of "aggression" or "cooperation" if one's measures of these terms confuse causally or functionally quite different kinds of behavior? Possible relationships more likely will be obscured than revealed.

The point discussed here is very simple, but difficult to communicate, perhaps because it turns the usual processes of social-behavior research upside down. It has long been a custom to start with a concept like "agression" and then look for a good measure(s) of it. For instance, Wright (1960), reviewing observational studies of child behavior, cites all the following terms as having been used quite uncritically: anger, outbreaks of fear, jealousy, conformity, competitive behavior, seeking affection, friendly approaches, seeking recognition, sociability. The traditional view is defended with a number of well-worn axioms like: "You can't measure everything," "Counting movements is like counting the leaves on a tree," or "We are not interested in superficial behavior but in the psychologically meaningful variables." Indeed the central issue is how these meaningful variables are to be determined. The position offered by ethologists and that supported in this volume is that psychologically meaningful variables are derived from data.

Briefly, the ethological method of response-category selection follows from a thorough descriptive period in which the temporal co-occurrence of specific motor patterns are recorded and analyzed in sequential fashion. For example, Blurton Jones (1972) has derived the category "smile" from the composite of the following motor patterns: oblong and upward curl of bottom and upper lip, teeth touching, visual orientation to playmates. The influence of this technique recently has been evidenced in applied-behavior analyses of social contacts among preschool children (e.g., Wahler, 1967). Although the initial recording of behavioral events was in terms of categories of activity (e.g., hits, looks) rather than discrete motor patterns, the final behavior categories (e.g., aggressive behavior, attending to aggression) nonetheless were determined from observations of *ongoing* child behaviors and their usual consequences.

A final aspect of observational methodology that is uniquely

treated by ethology is the perennial question of reliability. Ethologists generally have been skeptical of interobserver reliability as a
way of evaluating the validity of items to be recorded. This
skepticism is most closely related to the ethologist's experience
with a tradition of inter- rather than intraexperiment tests of
reliability. As was mentioned earlier, the determination of inter
observer agreements is a highly reactive process, in which the
accuracy and logical consistency of behavior-classification systems
are obfuscated by a number of observer and situational variables.
In an effort to separate observer and situational variables from the
adequacy of their observational systems, ethologists have used the
replicability of their studies as an index of reliability. According to
Blurton Jones (1972), "a worker in another laboratory on a different
continent can read the account of one ethologist and know exactly
what behavior to look for, and can therefore repeat earlier studies"
(p. 13). The ethologists' reliance on replication of studies may have
been encouraged by the assumption that the behavior of animals
did not vary greatly within a species. With the recent increase in
descriptions of apparent intertroop differences in various primate
species (see Crook, 1970, for summary) this assumption can no
longer be relied upon. However, interobserver reliability testing is
not a very useful solution to this problem. One team of observers
may agree together but disagree with an isolated team, and even if
the observers train together, they may diverge during the study
(Gewirtz & Gewirtz, 1969). The best solutions are either the one
that has been adopted where the observers of two differing
populations test each other's categories (replication), or the more
generous use of permanent records like film and videotape.
Clearly, both inter- and intraexperiment measures of reliability add
to the "believability" of research findings. In the ideal experimental program, both calculations would be made.

In summary, the ethological system of observing social behavior
provides a complete and exacting study of interactive behavior. Its
characteristics of extensive preliminary observation, unambiguous
behavior categories, sequential recording and analysis, and, most
important, the use of in vivo interactions as the principle unit of
behavior bring both internal and external validity to the method.
Although ethological studies of children's social behavior have
been largely descriptive and correlational, rather than analytic, an
exciting potential exists for "controlled" ethological investigations.

A logical intersection of methodologies proposed here would include an ethological measurement perspective on interactive behavior, coupled with experimental design tactics of applied behavior analysis as described by Baer, Wolf, and Risley (1968). Such a union would *not* compromise either perspective of social behavior; rather, it would highlight the strengths of each approach—the unit of measurement in ethology and the experimental control of behavior analysis.

Summary

For a theory of social behavior to be useful in unraveling the topographic and functional characteristics of interactive behavior, it must promote a dyadic unit of measurement. A principle concern in this chapter has been to focus attention upon the monadic, nonsocial behaviors that have been the scientific subject matter of much operant theory and research (e.g., Bandura, Ross, & Ross, 1963; Gewirtz & Baer, 1958a, b; Hart *et al.*, 1968). Such a methodology and orientation has persisted despite Sears' (1951) clear statement of the need for dyadic analyses in social-behavior research.

In their conceptualizations of interactive behaviors in a dyadic, response-support framework, Bell (1968, 1971, 1974), Cairns (1972), and Sears (1951) have provided a comprehensive theory and methodology for the integration of experimental and observational findings. In contrast to the social reinforcement paradigm, the dyadic response system has proven to be compatible with an analysis of interactional data. Fundamental to such an analysis is the specification of the "effective" stimulus for behavior. Within the dyadic response framework, individual responses are controlled not only by the behavior of the other but by the context in which the interaction occurs, the developmental status of the individuals, and their momentary endogenous states (Cairns, 1972).

This emphasis on dyadic, interactional units of measurement is again present in ethological conceptualizations of social behavior. The ethological approach to behavior measurement is unique, however, in its molecular analysis of gestures, postures, and visual fixations. Such an approach not only reduces the amount of observer inference in naturalistic data but also allows for a bio-physical, phylogenetic analysis of social-interaction patterns.

Finally, it has been proposed in this chapter that operant, dyadic, and ethological conceptualizations of social behavior have had a pervasive influence on direct-observational systems for analyzing preschool children's interactive behavior. Despite their conceptual and methodological weaknesses, diary records, time and event sampling, and ethological recording systems all have provided distinct contributions to the in vivo study of social behavior. The longitudinal perspective of diary records, the regularization of obeserver and recording instrument within time-sampling proce-dures, and the continuous observation of interactive sequences of behavior by ethological methods all are necessary in developing a comprehensive system for assessing social behaviors. The impor-tance of such an integrative approach cannot be too strongly emphasized, for continued interchanges can only foster a more coherent and unified science of social behavior.

REFERENCES

Adams, D. K. The development of social behavior. In Y. Brackbill (Ed.), *Infancy and early childhood.* New York: Free Press, 1967. Pp. 377–426.

Allport, F. H. *Social psychology.* Boston: Houghton, 1924.

Altmann, S. A. Sociobiology of rhesus. II. Stocastics of social communication. *Journal of Theoretical Biology,* 1965, *8,* 490–522.

Arrington, R. E. *Interrelations in the behavior of young children.* New York: Teachers College, 1932.

Arrington, R. E. Time sampling in studies of social behavior: A critical review of techniques and results with research suggestions. *Psychological Bulletin,* 1943, *40,* 81–124.

Baer, D. M., Peterson, R. F., & Sherman, J. A. Building an imitative repertoire by programming similarity between child and model as discriminative for rein-forcement. Paper read at biennial meeting of the Society for Research in Child Development, Minneapolis, Minnesota, March, 1965.

Baer, D. M., & Sherman, J. A. Reinforcement control of generalized imitation in young children. *Journal of Experimental Child Psychology,* 1964, *1,* 37–49.

Baer, D. M., Wolf, M. M., & Risley, T. R. Some current dimensions of applied behavior analysis. *Journal of Applied Behavior Analysis,* 1968, *1,* 91–97.

Bandura, A. Vicarious processes: A case of no-trial learning. In L. Berkowitz (Ed.), *Advances in experimental social psychology.* Vol. 2. New York: Academic Press, 1965. Pp. 1–55.

Bandura, A. *Principles of behavior modification.* New York: Holt, 1969.

Bandura, A., Grusec, J. E., & Menlove, F. L. The influence of symbolization and incentive set on observational learning. *Child Development,* 1966, *37,* 499–506.

Bandura, A., & Kupers, C. J. Transmission of patterns of self-reinforcement through modeling. *Journal of Abnormal and Social Psychology,* 1964, *69,* 1–9.

Bandura, A., Ross, D., & Ross, S. A. Imitation of film-mediated agressive models. *Journal of Abnormal and Social Psychology,* 1963, *66,* 3–11.

Bandura, A., & Walters, R. H. *Social learning and personality development.* New York: Holt, 1963.

Barker, M. *A technique for studying the social-material activities of young children.* New York: Columbia Univ. Press, 1930.

Baron, R. M. Social reinforcement effects as a function of social reinforcement history. *Psychological Review,* 1966, *73,* 527–539.

Beach, F. A., & Jaynes, J. Studies of maternal retrieving in rats. Sensory cues involved in the lactating female's response to her young. *Behavior,* 1965, *10,* 104–125.

Beaver, A. P. *The initiation of social contacts by preschool children: A study of technique in recording social behavior.* New York: Teachers College, 1932.

Bell, R. Q. A reinterpretation of the direction of effects in studies of socialization. *Psychological Review,* 1968, *75,* 81–95.

Bell, R. Q. Stimulus control of parent or caretaker behavior by offspring. *Developmental Psychology,* 1971, *4,* 63–72.

Bell, R. Q. Contributions of human infants to caregiving and social interaction. In M. Lewis & L. A. Rosenblum (Eds.), *The effect of the infant on its caregiver.* New York: Wiley, 1974. Pp. 1–19.

Berkowitz, H., Butterfield, E. C., & Zigler, E. The effectiveness of social reinforcers on persistence and learning tasks following positive and negative social interactions. *Journal of Personality and Social Psychology,* 1965, *2,* 706–714.

Berkowitz, H., & Zigler, E. Effects of preliminary positive and negative interactions and delay conditions on children's responsiveness to social reinforcement. *Journal of Personality and Social Psychology,* 1962, *2,* 500–505.

Bijou, S. W., & Baer, D. M. Some methodological contributions from a functional analysis of child development. In L. P. Lipsitt & C. C. Spiker (Eds.), *Advances in child development and behavior.* Vol. 1. New York: Academic Press, 1963. Pp. 197–231.

Bijou, S. W., & Baer, D. M. *Child development* Vol. 2. *Universal stage of infancy.* New York: Appleton, 1965.

Bijou, S. W., Peterson, R. F., & Ault, M. H. A method to integrate descriptive and experimental field studies at the level of data and empirical concepts. *Journal of Applied Behavior Analysis,* 1968, *1,* 175–191.

Bijou, S. W., Peterson, R. F., Harris, F. R., Allen, K. E., & Johnston, M. S. Methodology for experimental studies of young children in natural settings. *Psychological Record,* 1969, *19,* 177–210.

Blurton Jones, N. G. *Ethological studies of child behavior.* London: Cambridge Univ. Press, 1972.

Bobbitt, R. A., Jensen, G. D., & Kuehn, R. E. Development and application of an observational method: A pilot study of the mother–infant relationship in pigtail monkeys. *Journal of Genetic Psychology,* 1964, *105,* 257–274.

Bott, H. Observations of play activities in nursery school. *Genetic Psychology Monographs,* 1928, *4,* 44–88.

Brackbill, Y. Extinction of the smiling response in infants as a function of reinforcement schedule. *Child Development*, 1958, *29*, 115–124.

Brannigan, C. R., & Humphries, D. A. Human non-verbal behavior, a means of communication. In N. Blurton Jones (Ed.), *Ethological studies of child behavior*. London: Cambridge Univ. Press, 1972. Pp. 37–64.

Buell, J., Stoddard, P., Harris, F. R., & Baer, D. M. Collateral social development accompanying reinforcement of outdoors play in a preschool child. *Journal of Applied Behavior Analysis*, 1968, *1*, 167–174.

Butler, R. A., & Harlow, H. F. Persistence of visual explorations in monkeys. *Journal of Comparative and Physiological Psychology*, 1954, *47*, 258–263.

Butterfield, E. C., & Zigler, E. The effects of differing institutional climates on the effectiveness of social reinforcement in the mentally retarded. *American Journal of Mental Deficiency*, 1965, *70*, 45–56.

Cairns, R. B. Antecedents of social reinforcer effectiveness. Unpublished manuscript, Indiana Univ., 1963.

Cairns, R. B. Attachment behavior of mammals,. *Psychological Review*, 1966, *73*, 409–426.

Cairns, R. B. The informational properties of verbal and nonverbal events. *Journal of Personality and Social Psychology*, 1967, *5*, 353–357.

Cairns, R. B. Attachment and dependency: A psychobiological and social-learning synthesis. In J. L. Gewirtz (Ed.), *Attachment and dependency*. Washington, D.C.: V. H. Winston, 1972. Pp. 29–80.

Cohen. A. R., Greenbaum, C. W., & Mansson, H. H. Commitment to social deprivation and verbal conditioning. *Journal of Abnormal and Social Psychology*, 1963, *67*, 410–421.

Creak, M. The schizophrenic syndrome in childhood. *British Medical Journal*, 1961, *2*, 889.

Crook, J. H. Social organization and the environment: Aspects of contemporary social ethology. *Animal Behavior*, 1970, *18*, 197–209.

Curry, C. The effects of verbal reinforcement combinations on learning in children. *Journal of Experimental Psychology*, 1960, *59*, 434.

Dawe, H. C. An analysis of two hundred quarrels of preschool children. *Child Development*, 1934, *5*, 139–157.

Dewey, J., & Bentley, A. F. *Knowing and the known*. Boston: Beacon Press, 1949.

Dinsmoor, J. A. Comments on Wetzel's treatment of a case of compulsive stealing. *Journal of Consulting Psychology*, 1966, *30*, 378–380.

Dollard, J., & Miller, N. E. *Personality and psychotherapy*. New York: McGraw-Hill, 1950.

Eisenberger, R. Is there a deprivation–satiation function for social approval? *Psychological Bulletin*, 1970, *74*, 255–275.

Endo, G. T. Social drive or arousal: A test of two theories of social isolation. *Journal of Experimental Child Psychology,*, 1968, *6*, 61–74.

Epstein, W. Experimental investigations of the genesis of visual space perception. *Psychological Bulletin*, 1964, *61*, 115–128.

Gelfand, D., & Hartmann, D. P. Behavior therapy with children: A review and evaluation of research methodology. *Psychological Bulletin*, 1968, *69*, 204–215.

Gellert, E. Systematic observation: A method of child study. *Harvard Educational Review*, 1955, *25*, 179–195.

Gewirtz, J. L. Potency of a social reinforcer as a function of satiation and recovery. *Developmental Psychology*, 1969, *1*, 2–13.

Gewirtz, J. L., & Baer, D. M. Deprivation and satiation of social reinforcers as drive conditions. *Journal of Abnormal and Social Psychology*, 1958, *57*, 165–172. (a)

Gewirtz, J. L., & Baer, D. M. The effect of brief social deprivation on behaviors for a social reinforcer. *Journal of Abnormal and Social Psychology*, 1958, *56*, 49–56. (b)

Gewirtz, H. B., & Gewirtz, J. L. Caretaking settings, background events and behavior differences in four Israeli child-rearing environments: Some preliminary trends. In B. M. Foss (Ed.), *Determinants of infant behavior*. Vol. 4. London: Methuen, 1969. Pp. 229–252.

Grant, E. C. Analysis of the social behavior of the male laboratory rat. *Behavior*, 1963, *21*, 260–281.

Green, E. H. Group play and quarreling among preschool children. *Child Development*, 1933, *4*, 302–307.

Grossman, B. Parental warmth, child dependency, and responsiveness to social reinforcement. Unpublished doctoral dissertation, Duke Univ., 1963.

Hart, B. M., Reynolds, N. J., Baer, D. M., Brawley, E. R., & Harris, F. R. Effect of contingent and noncontingent social reinforcement on the cooperative play of a preschool child. *Journal of Applied Behavior Analysis*, 1968, *1*, 73–76.

Hartup, W. W. Nurturance and nurturance-withdrawal in relation to the dependency behavior of preschool children. *Child Development*, 1958, *29*, 191–201.

Hartup, W. W. Friendship status and the effectiveness of peers as reinforcing agents. *Journal of Experimental Child Psychology*, 1964, *1*, 154–162.

Hartup, W. W. Peer interaction and social organization. In P. H. Mussen (Ed.), *Carmichael's manual of child psychology*. Vol. 2. New York: Wiley, 1970. Pp. 361–456.

Hartup, W. W., & Himeno, Y. Social isolation vs. interaction with adults in relation to aggression in preschool children. *Journal of Abnormal and Social Psychology*, 1959, *59*, 17–22.

Hawkins, R. P., Peterson, R. F., Schweid, E., & Bijou, S. W. Behavior therapy in the home: Ameliorating of problem parent–child relations with the parent in a therapeutic role. *Journal of Experimental Child Psychology*, 1966, *4*, 99–107.

Hinde, R. A. Unitary drives. *Animal behavior*, 1959, *7*, 130–141.

Holt, C. B. *Animal drive and the learning process*. Vol. 1. New York: Holt, 1931.

Humphrey, C. Imitation and the conditioned reflex. *Pedagogical Seminary*, 1921, *28*, 1–21.

Hutt, C., & Ounsted, C. The biological significance of gaze aversion with particular reference to the syndrome of infantile autism. *Behavioral Science*, 1966, *11*, 346–356.

Hutt, C., & Vaizey, M. J. Differential effects of group density on social behavior. *Nature*, 1966, *209*, 1371–1372.

Hutt, S. J., & Hutt, C. *Direct observation and measurement of behavior*. Springfield, Illinois: Charles C. Thomas, 1970.

Jersild, A. T., & Fite, M. D. *Children's social adjustments in nursery school*. New York: Teachers College, 1937.

Kirby, F. D., & Toler, H. C. Modification of preschool isolate behavior: A case study. *Journal of Applied Behavior Analysis*, 1970, *3*, 309–314.

Kopfstein, D. Effects of accelerating and decelerating consequences on the social behavior of trainable retarded children. *Child Development*, 1972, *43*, 800–809.

Kozma, A. The effects of anxiety, stimulation, and isolation on social reinforcer effectiveness. *Journal of Experimental Child Psychology*, 1969, *8*, 1–8.

Landau, R., & Gewirtz, J. L. Differential satiation for a social reinforcing stimulus as a determinant of its efficacy in conditioning. *Journal of Experimental Child Psychology*, 1967, *5*, 391–405.

Lasko, J. K. Parent behavior toward first and second children. *Genetic Psychology Monographs*, 1954, *49*, 97–137.

Lehrman, D. A critique of Konrad Larenz's theory of instinctive behavior. *Quarterly Review of Biology*, 1953, *28*, 337–363.

Levy, D. M. *Behavioral analysis: Analysis of clinical observations of behavior as applied to mother–newborn relationships.* New York: Charles C. Thomas, 1958.

Lewis, M. Social isolation: A parametric study of its effect on social reinforcement. *Journal of Experimental Child Psychology*, 1965, *2*, 205–218.

Lewis, M., & Richman, S. Social encounters and their effect on subsequent social reinforcement. *Journal of Abnormal and Social Psychology*, 1964, *69*, 253–257.

Lindsley, O. R. Experimental analysis of cooperation and competition. In T. Verhave (Ed.), *The experimental analysis of behavior.* New York: Appleton, 1966. Pp. 470–501.

Lipsitt, L. P. Learning in the human infant. In H. W. Stevenson, E. H. Hess, & H. L. Rheingold (Eds.), *Early behavior: Comparative and developmental approaches.* New York: Wiley, 1967. Pp. 147–180.

Lovaas, O. I., Berberich, J. P., Perloff, B. F., & Schaeffer, B. Acquisition of imitative speech by schizophrenic children. *Science*, 1966, *151*, 705–707.

Lundin, R. W. *Personality: An experimental approach.* New York: Macmillan, 1961.

Mallay, H. A. A study of some of the techniques underlying the establishment of successful social contacts at the preschool level. *Journal of Genetic Psychology*, 1935, *47*, 431–457.

Marshall, H. R., & Hahn, S. C. Experimental modification of dramatic play. *Journal of Personality and Social Psychology*, 1967, *5*, 119–122.

McCullers, J. C., & Stevenson, H. W. Effects of verbal reinforcement in a probability learning situation. *Psychological Reports*, 1960, *7*, 439–445.

McDougall, W. *An introduction to social psychology.* London: Methuen, 1908.

McGrew, W. C. Aspects of social development in nursery school children, with emphasis on introduction to the group. In N. Blurton Jones (Ed.), *Ethological studies of child behavior.* London: Cambridge Univ. Press, 1972. Pp. 129–156.

Medley, D. M., & Mitzel, H. E. Measuring classroom behavior by systematic observations. In N. L. Gage (Ed.), *Handbook of research on teaching.* Chicago: Rand McNally, 1963. Pp. 247–328.

Metz, J. R. Conditioning generalized imitation in autistic children. *Journal of Experimental Child Psychology*, 1965, *2*, 389–397.

Miller, N. E. The frustration–agression hypothesis. *Psychological Review*, 1941, *48*, 337–342.

Miller, N. E., & Dollard, J. *Social learning and imitation.* New Haven: Yale Univ. Press, 1941.

Mischel, W. *Personality and assessment.* New York: Wiley, 1968.

Morgan, C. L. *Habit and instinct.* London: Arnold, 1896.

Mowrer, O. H. *Learning theory and personality dynamics.* New York: Ronald, 1950.

O'Connor, R. D. Modification of social withdrawal through symbolic modeling. *Journal of Applied Behavior Analysis,* 1969, *2,* 15–22.

Paris, S. G., & Cairns, R. B. An experimental and ethological analysis of social reinforcement with retarded children. *Child Development,* 1972, *43,* 717–729.

Parke, R. D. (Ed.) *Readings in social development.* New York: Holt, 1969.

Parten, M. B. Social participation among preschool children. *Journal of Abnormal and Social Psychology,* 1932, *27,* 243–269.

Parton, D. A., & Ross, A. O. Social reinforcement of children's motor behavior: A review. *Psychological Bulletin,* 1965, *64,* 65–73.

Parton, D. A., & Ross, A. O. A reply to "the use of rate as a measure of response in studies of social reinforcement." *Psychological Bulletin,* 1967, *67,* 323–325.

Patterson, G. R. Manual for the behavior rating sheet. (4th ed.) Unpublished manuscript, Oregon Research Institute, 1967.

Patterson, G. R., & Cobb, J. A. A dyadic analysis of "aggressive" behaviors. Paper presented at the 5th Minnesota Symposium on Child Psychology, Minneapolis, May, 1970.

Patterson, G. R., & Hinsey, W. C. Investigations of some assumptions and characteristics of a procedure for instrumental conditioning in children. *Journal of Experimental Child Psychology,* 1964, *1,* 111–122.

Raush, H. L. Interaction sequences. *Journal of Personality and Social Psychology,* 1965, *2,* 487–499.

Ray, J. S. Behavior of developmentally delayed and nondelayed toddler-age children: An ethological study. Unpublished doctoral dissertation, George Peabody College, 1974.

Reid, J. B. Reliabity assessment of observational data: A possible methodological problem. *Child Development,* 1970, *41,* 1143–1150.

Rheingold, H. L. (Ed.) *Maternal behavior in mammals.* New York: Wiley, 1963.

Rheingold, H. L. The development of social behavior in the human infant. In H. W. Stevenson (Ed.), Concept of development: A report of a conference commemorating the fortieth anniversary of the Institute of Child Development, Univ. of Minnesota. *Monographs of the Society for Research in Child Development,* 1966, *31,* (5, Whole No. 107).

Rheingold, H. L., Gewirtz, J. L., & Ross, H. W. Social conditioning of vocalizations in infants. *Journal of Comparative Physiological Psychology,* 1959, *52,* 68–73.

Romanczyk, R. G., Kent, R. N., Diament, C., & O'Leary, K. O. Measuring the reliability of observational data: A reactive process. *Journal of Applied Behavior Analysis,* 1973, *6,* 175–184.

Rotter, J. B. *Social learning and clinical psychology.* Englewood Cliffs, New Jersey: Prentice-Hall, 1954.

Satinoff, E., & Stanely, W. C. Effect of stomach loading on sucking behavior in neonatal puppies. *Journal of Comparative and Physiological Psychology,* 1963, *56,* 66–68.

Schaefer, E. Parent–child interactional patterns and parental attitudes. In D. Rosenthal (Ed.), *The Genain quadruplets.* New York: Basic Books, 1963. Pp. 398–430.

Scheflen, A. E. The significance of posture in communication systems. *Psychiatry,* 1963, *26,* 316–331.

Schmitt, D. R., & Marwell, G. Stimulus control in the experimental study of cooperation. *Journal of the Experimental Analysis of Behavior*, 1968, *11*, 571–574.

Schmitt, D. R., & Marwell, G. Taking and the disruption of cooperation. *Journal of the Experimental Analysis of Behavior*, 1971, *15*, 405–412.

Sears, R. R. A theoretical framework for personality and social behavior. *American Psychologist*, 1951, *6*, 476–483.

Sears, R. R., Maccoby, E. E., & Levin, H. *Patterns of child rearing.* Evanston, Illinois: Row, Peterson, 1957.

Skinner, B. F. *The behavior of organisms.* New York: Appleton, 1938.

Skinner, B. F. *Science and human behavior.* New York: Macmillan, 1953.

Smith, P. K., & Connolly, K. Patterns of play and social interaction in pre-school children. In N. Blurton Jones (Ed.), *Ethological studies of child behavior.* London: Cambridge Univ. Press, 1972. Pp. 65–96.

Solomon, R. W., & Wahler, R. G. Peer reinforcement control of classroom problem behavior. *Journal of Applied Behavior Analysis*, 1973, *6*, 49–56.

Spence, J. T. Verbal discrimination performance as a function of instructions and verbal reinforcement combination in normal and retarded children. *Child Development*, 1966, *37*, 269–281.

Stern, D. N. Mother and infant at play: The dyadic interaction involving facial, vocal, and gaze behaviors. In M. Lewis & L. Rosenblum (Eds.), *The effect of the infant on its caregiver.* New York: Wiley, 1974.

Stevenson, H. W. Social reinforcement with children as a function of CA, sex of E and sex of S. *Journal of Abnormal and Social Psychology*, 1961, *63*, 147–154.

Steveson, H. W. Social reinforcement of children's behavior. In L. P. Lipsitt & C. C. Spiker (Eds.), *Advances in child development.* Vol. 2. New York: Academic Press, 1965. Pp. 97–126.

Stevenson, H. W., & Fahel, L. S. The effect of social reinforcement on the performance of institutionalized and noninstitutionalized normal and feeble-minded children. *Journal of Personality*, 1961, *29*, 136–147.

Stevenson, H. W., & Hill, K. The effect of social reinforcement following success and failure. Unpublished manuscript, Univ. of Minnesota, 1963.

Stevenson, H. W., Keen, R., & Knights, R. M. Parents and strangers as reinforcing agents for children's performance. *Journal of Abnormal and Social Psychology*, 1963, *67*, 183–186.

Stevenson, H. W., & Knights, R. M. Social reinforcement with normal and retarded children as a function of pretraining, sex of E, and sex of S. *American Journal of Mental Deficiency*, 1962, *66*, 866–871.

Stevenson, H. W., & Odom, R. D. The effectiveness of social reinforcement following two conditions of social deprivation. *Journal of Abnormal and Social Psychology*, 1962, *65*, 429–431.

Stott, L. H. Parent–adolescent adjustment: Its measurement and significance. *Character and Personality*, 1941, *10*, 140–150.

Strain, B. A. Early dialogues: A naturalistic study of vocal behavior in mothers and three month old infants. Unpublished doctoral dissertation, George Peabody College, Nashville, Tennessee, 1974.

Strain, P. S., & Timm, M. A. An experimental analysis of social interaction between a behaviorally disordered preschool child and her classroom peers. *Journal of Applied Behavior Analysis*, 1974, *7*, 583–590.

Swift, J. Effects of early group experience: The nursery school and day nursery. In M. L. Hoffman & L. W. Hoffman (Eds.), *Review of child development research.* Vol. 1. New York: Russell Sage Foundation, 1964. Pp. 249–288.

Symmes, D. Anxiety reduction and novelty as goals of visual exploration by monkeys. *Journal of Genetic Psychology,* 1959, *94,* 181–198.

Thoman, E., Wetzel, A., & Levine, S. Learning in the neonate rat. *Animal Behavior,* 1968, *16,* 54–57.

Tinbergen, N. *The study of instinct.* London: Oxford Univ. Press, 1951.

Updegraff, R., & Herbst, E. K. An experimental study of the social behavior stimulated in young children by certain play materials. *Journal of Genetic Psychology,* 1933, *42,* 372–391.

Van Alstyne, D. *Play behavior and choice of play materials of preschool children.* Chicago: Univ. of Chicago Press, 1932.

Wahler, R. G. Child–child interaction in a free-field setting: Some experimental analyses. *Journal of Experimental Child Psychology,* 1967, *5,* 278–293.

Wahler, R. G., Winkel, G. H., Peterson, R. F., & Morrison, D. C. Mothers as behavior therapists for their own children. *Behavior Research and Therapy,* 1965, *3,* 113–124.

Walters, R. H., & Karal, P. Social deprivation and verbal behavior. *Journal of Personality,* 1960, *28,* 89–107.

Walters, R. H., Marshall, W. E., & Shooter, J. R. Anxiety, isolation, and susceptibility to social influence. *Journal of Personality,* 1960, *28,* 518–529.

Walters, R. H., & Parke, R. D. Emotional arousal, isolation and discrimination learning in children. *Journal of Experimental Child Psychology,* 1964, *1,* 163–173.

Walters, R. H., & Parke, R. D. The role of the distance receptors in the development of social responsiveness. In L. P. Lipsitt & C. C. Spiker (Eds.), *Advances in child development and behavior.* Vol. 2. New York: Academic Press, 1965. Pp. 59–96.

Walters, R. H., & Ray, E. Anxiety, social isolation and reinforcer effectiveness. *Journal of Personality,* 1960, *28,* 359–367.

Wright, H. F. Observational child study. In P. H. Mussen (Ed.), *Handbook of research methods in child development.* New York: Wiley, 1960. Pp. 71–139.

Wright, H. F. *Recording and analyzing child behavior.* New York: Harper, 1967.

Yarrow, L. J. Research in dimensions of early maternal care. *Merrill-Palmer Quarterly,* 1963, *9,* 101–114.

Zigler, E. Rigidity and social reinforcement effects in the performance of institutionalized and noninstitutionalized normal and retarded children. *Journal of Personality,* 1963, *31,* 258–269.

Zigler, E., & Kanzer, P. The effectiveness of two classes of verbal reinforcers on the performance of middle and lower income class children. *Journal of Personality,* 1962, *30,* 157–163.

Introduction

Some children have difficulty learning to relate in a reciprocally reinforcing manner with their peers (Patterson & Reid, 1969). This chapter concerns one such population, the "socially withdrawn." The socially withdrawn may be operationally defined as those children who demonstrate low rates of social behavior in interaction with peers (Kale, Kaye, Whelan, & Hopkins, 1968). Various descriptors have been used in the educational and psychological literature to designate  this population, for example, the "socially isolated" (Kirby & Toler, 1970), the "anxious-withdrawn" (Quay, 1969), the "isolate" (Amidon, 1961) or, simply, the "introvert" (Clement, 1967). From a learning-theory perspective, the socially withdrawn are those individuals who, owing to response deficits and/or stimulus-control deficiencies, infrequently engage in mutually reinforcing interactions with their peers. O'Connor (1972) provided evidence indicating that, in free-play settings, the typical preschool-age child interacts with peers approximately 21% to 32% of the time. O'Connor suggested that children who interact with peers less than 15% of the time in such situations should be considered "isolates" and provided appropriate educational therapy.

In this chapter, the term "social withdrawal" is used as a descriptor for individuals who (owing to constitutional and/or experiential deficits) demonstrate social performance judged deficient by social agents (e.g., parents and teachers) controlling the reinforcers available in their environment. The term describes a pattern of behavior that cuts across traditional categories of exceptionality, such as autism, mental retardation, and schizophrenia. The identification of behavior as socially withdrawn rests upon the following criteria: (1) the occurrence of social behavior with peers as measured by its frequency, intensity, and/or duration; (2) the number of peers with whom interaction occurs; and (3) the extent to which social interaction can be maintained in a natural environmental setting.

Socially withdrawn behavior may be further classified with respect to a bipolar continuum that ranges from Type I, deficient social repertoire, to Type II, deficient social performance. Type I behavior is demonstrated by children who, in an environmental setting suitable for the maintenance of most children's social behavior, consistently exhibit a limited number of social-response topographies. Moreover, their topographies are emitted at low rates, and are frequently not under the stimulus control of peer behavior. In some extreme cases, human attention does not function as a generalized conditioned reinforcer with Type I children (Lovaas, Freitag, Kinder, Rubenstein, Schaeffer, & Simmons, 1964). Type I children's deficient social behavior is frequently accompanied by other assessed deficits, such as motor, intellectual, and/or language delays (e.g., Whitman, Mercurio, & Caponigri, 1970). The distinguishing characteristic of Type I children is that they have not acquired the basic vocal and motor-response topographies necessary for mutually reinforcing interactions with peers. Children classified under Type II social performance are capable of demonstrating a variety of adaptive responses in peer interactions but rarely emit social responses and/or emit social responses only in the presence of certain people (e.g., with teachers but not with peers [Hart, Reynolds, Baer, Brawley, & Harris, 1968] or with opposite-sex peers but not same-sex peers [Sibley, Abbott, Stark, Bullock, & Leonhardt, 1967]). Thus, Type II children are those who possess the necessary behavioral repertoire for interaction but, nonetheless, do not interact with peers.

This chapter is written to accomplish two primary purposes. First, it evaluates the significance of the problem of childhood social withdrawal. Secondly, it critically reviews existing classroom procedures for modifying Type II withdrawn children's social interaction. Several procedural suggestions appear in the course of this review.

Significance of the Problem

This section of the chapter evaluates the significance of the problem of childhood social withdrawal. First, it considers evidence attesting that social agents (i.e., parents and teachers) consider social withdrawal a deviant pattern of behavior. Next, it notes certain theoretical and empirical support for the position that childhood social withdrawal is a response pattern frequently associated with developmental delays. Finally, it reviews correlational studies bearing on the relationship between childhood social withdrawal and adult schizophrenia.

SOCIAL AGENTS' PERSPECTIVES OF CHILDHOOD SOCIAL WITHDRAWAL

Descriptive studies of childhood characteristics labeled "atypical" in American culture have indicated consistently that social agents consider social withdrawal an expression of deviancy. These studies have shown that 14% to 30% of those youngsters whom social agents consider "problem children" are termed "problems" because they demonstrate low rates of social performance. Gilbert (1957), for example, categorized casefolder information on 2500 referrals to 4 urban child-guidance centers. He found passive or withdrawn behavior to be a presenting problem in approximately 15% of referrals on children under 6 years old. He noted that this figure decreased to 12% when all ages, birth through 18 years, were considered. In another study, Rogers, Lilenfield, and Pasamanick (1955) analyzed the frequency with which particular categories of unacceptable behavior were reported by elementary school teachers. They found social withdrawal to be major presenting complaint in 15% of cases. Woody (1964) studied the behavioral characteristics of preadolescent-age problem children identified through teacher referrals. He observed that 14% of such referrals were children termed "withdrawn." Finally, Heinstein (1969) presented a list of childhood behavior problems to a sample of California mothers, asking them to indicate the deviant characteristics they perceived in their children. Of a sample of 142 mothers of 5-year-olds, 30% indicated that they viewed their children as being too "shy." Considered cumulatively, these studies demonstrate that social withdrawal is considered a deviant pattern of behavior by social agents, and that it represents a major presenting symptom in 15% or more of cases in which youngsters are referred for psychological services.

RELATIONSHIP OF CHILDHOOD SOCIAL WITHDRAWAL TO OTHER DEVELOPMENTAL AND EDUCATIONAL PROBLEMS

Child developmentalists widely have recognized the importance to development of satisfying early peer contacts. Cooley (1909) wrote that, "without healthy play, especially group play, human nature cannot rightly develop" (p. 49). More recent commentators also supported this position. Blurton Jones (1967) hypothesized that early play experience with peers may be as important for human development as Harlow and Harlow (1962) found it to be for the development of adaptive social and sexual behavior among rhesus monkeys. McCandless and Hoyt (1961) have posited that peer interaction among preschool-age children is indispensible for normal development. These authors maintained that peer interaction provides children with otherwise unobtainable opportunities to rehearse important life roles. Similarly, Reese and Lipsitt (1970) emphasized the influence of peer behavior on human development. They stressed that early peer interaction is of profound developmental significance because it provides children with contexts for practicing motor, language, and social skills essential for normal adult functioning.

Social withdrawal may be a performance pattern that frequently begins in the preschool years and persists over lengthy periods, perhaps throughout life (Morris, Soroker, & Burrus, 1954). Research has shown that children's degrees of peer interaction generally stabilize during the preschool years (Challman, 1932; Green, 1933; Parten, 1933), with mutually congenial children pairing off into relationships that exclude, among others, passive children (Sorokin & Grove, 1950). Some evidence indicated long-term consistency in attained levels of social participation (Van Alstyne & Hattwick, 1939) and peer-group acceptance (Singer, 1951). Bonney (1943), Moreno (1934), and Ausubel (1958) each noted consistency in the nature of social interaction and warned that children not accepted by their peers in the early grades will have considerable difficulty developing satisfying interpersonal relationships as adults.

Evidence of the relationship between social withdrawal, delayed cognitive development, and impaired academic performance has appeared in the child development literature. Piaget (Piaget & Inhelder, 1969) theorized that the age at which children demonstrate behaviors characteristic of various periods or stages of cognitive development depends, to a large degree, on the nature and extent of their social interaction. Piaget stressed that cognitive and social aspects of behavioral development are inseparable. Empirical evidence in direct support of Piaget's position is scarce, but some research is available. Rardin and Moan (1971) examined the extent of correlation in the development of assessed aspects of cognitive and social development among kindergarten, first-, second-, and third-grade children. Their results indicated that children demonstrate similar developmental progressions in their cognitive and social domains. Rardin and Moan interpreted this as suggesting that cognitive and social development parallel one another and possibly represent interdependent processes. In Hartup's (1970) words:

> There is little doubt that the changes which occur in child–child interactions during infancy and childhood are closely linked with changes in sensory-motor capacities, cognitive skills, and the development of impulse controls. [p. 368]

Other commentators noted that socially withdrawn children were likely to be low achievers in school (Bonney, 1971; Buswell, 1953), and that they often exhibited learning difficulties (Amidon & Hoffman, 1965). This characteristically poor academic performance by socially withdrawn children may be, in part, a result of restrictions in sensory stimulation associated with low social-performance levels. Inadequate peer stimulation in early childhood may result in a failure to develop those discriminations and response differentiations that are necessary prerequisites for successful school performance. There has been presented empirical evidence suggesting that children learn effectively when their learning experience involves peer interaction. Harris and Sherman (1973) found that peer–peer tutorial sessions held immediately prior to math classes resulted in improved accuracy and increased performance rates. Cobb (1970) reported that on-task conversation about academic materials by peers resulted in greater achievement gains than did individual attention to task. Children probably learn much through interaction with one another. The fact that socially withdrawn children receive little peer stimulation may explain their typically depressed academic-performance levels. Thus, the link between social withdrawal and developmental deficits in a number of areas seems well-established. As Whitman et al. (1970) stated the issue:

> Because many skills and discriminations are learned in a context of interpersonal reinforcement, social interaction is a critical prerequisite

for much of a child's behavioral development. Conversely, the absence of social interaction probably insures that development will be retarded. [p. 133]

Or, as Ausubel (1958) wrote:

If the opportunity for social experience is sufficiently curtailed, it interferes with the acquisition of necessary skills of communication, self assertion, and self defense and with the enactment of realistic and effective interpersonal roles during adolescence and adulthood. [p. 462]

RELATIONSHIP OF CHILDHOOD SOCIAL WITHDRAWAL TO ADULT BEHAVIORAL ABNORMALITY

Another line of research bearing on the significance of the problem of childhood social withdrawal has appeared over the past several decades in the psychiatric literature. These studies employed two type of correlational designs to test the hypothesis that childhood social withdrawal is related to adult schizophrenia. First, retrospective studies were reported on childhood behavior patterns demonstrated by adult schizophrenics (Birren, 1944; Bower, Shellhamer, & Daily, 1960; Bowman, 1934; Frazee, 1953; Kasanin & Veo, 1932; O'Neal & Robins, 1958; Wittman & Steinberg, 1944). Secondly, follow-up studies were presented regarding the proportion of socially withdrawn children subsequently labeled "schizophrenic" as adults (Michael, Morris , & Soroker, 1957; Morris et al., 1954; Robins, 1966). In retrospective studies, the general procedure was to identify populations of schizophrenic and nonschizophrenic adults and compare their childhood behavior patterns. Indices of the subjects' childhood behavior were determined through interviews with family members and acquaintances, and through inspection of educational and psychological case-history records. The procedure in follow-up studies was to compare the adult functioning of individuals considered withdrawn during childhood with those not so identified.

Retrospective investigations of the early behavior of adult psychotics consistently revealed social withdrawal as a characteristic noted in their behavioral histories. Kasanin and Veo (1932), for example, studied the school histories of children who later became schizophrenic to determine whether or not they differed in any discernible manner from their normally adjusted peers. School records, teacher interviews, and parent interviews constituted the data for the study. The authors reported that 28% of the 54 adult psychotics studied were characterized as "very sensitive, shy, bashful, passive boys or girls . . . [who] kept away as much as possible from the teachers and other children" (p. 221). The authors continued with,

> These children were so seclusive, and made so very few friends, or no friends at all, that we could not find any chums of theirs, for the simple reason that they had no chums. [p. 221]

In a similar study, Bowan (1934) compared information concerning the prepsychotic personalities of 322 mental patients to similar data on 96 normal comparison subjects. From an examination of 40 personality traits, Bowman concluded that, as distinguished from comparison subjects, "the schizophrenic tends to be a model child, to have few friends, to indulge in solitary amusements, to be a follower, to feel superior, to be closed mouthed and uncommunicative" (p. 497), or, in other words, to be a socially withdrawn child.

In another study, Birren (1944) classified 38 adult mental patients and 53 normal comparison subjects on the basis of an examiner's rating of their childhood reaction to a psychological test situation. Most adult schizophrenics were reported to have been withdrawn and apathetic during testing. Moreover, after comparing the schizophrenic subjects' hospital records with their earlier reactions to the testing situation, Birren concluded that

> an apathetic type of reaction in childhood is a relatively permanent type of behavior and is a forerunner of early hospitalization, poor hospital adjustment, and poor prognosis for recovery in cases developing mental disease. [p. 94]

Support for Birren's (1944) finding was supplied by Wittman and Steinberg (1944) and by Frazee (1953). Wittman and Steinberg inspected records of the childhood psychological test-session behavior of 33 adult schizophrenic mental patients and simlar data on

200 comparison subjects. They reported that

> more than 50% of the schizophrenic patients when examined as children were described by the psychologist at the time in terms of a shut-in personality type. [p. 814]

Frazee (1953) assessed records of the childhood behavior patterns of 23 adult schizophrenics (study group) and similar records of 23 nonschizophrenic adults (control group). The subjects in both groups were first seen when they were between 5 and 16 years of age at a center for behavior-disordered children. The experimenter was interested in determining if the study group differed from the control group at the time of their referral. Their central conclusion was that

> the children in the study group displayed a larger number of symptoms that could be classed as "withdrawn" and of greater severity than noted for the control group. [p. 121]

Of the 23 subjects in each group,

> twelve boys in the study group were said to have no friends and to be isolated from their own age group as compared with only five boys so described in the control group. Nine of the latter group were said to interact normally with other children while none of the study group evidenced anything approaching normal associations with other children. [p. 135]

The evidence thus far reviewed suggests the hypothesis that a significant positive relationship exists between adult schizophrenia and childhood social withdrawal. A study by O'Neal and Robins (1958), however, provided contradictory findings. These investigators compared the childhood behavioral histories of 28 adult schizophrenics with similar data on 57 normal adults. Descriptive data on both groups were recorded 27 to 32 years previous at the St. Louis Municipal Psychiatric Clinic when the subjects were in their early teens. O'Neal and Robins did not find social withdrawal to be an antecedent behavior pattern frequently noted in the childhood behavioral histories of their adult schizophrenic sample.

Bower et al. (1960) offered several explanations to account for the discrepancy between O'Neal and Robins' (1958) findings and those reported in previous retrospective investigations. First, the withdrawn group seen by O'Neal and Robins may have been "healthier" or have had more environmental supports than previous populations studied. Secondly, differential subject mortality (Campbell & Stanley, 1963) among schizophrenia-prone, withdrawn individuals may have operated as a confounding variable. This explanation seems highly tenable considering the results of another study by Robins and O'Neal (1958) in which the geographic mobility of disturbed subjects significantly exceeded that of control subjects. Thirdly, Bower et al. (1960) commented that O'Neal and Robins' (1958) schizophrenic subjects were identified on the basis of having had "difficulty with the law," a selection criterion not applied in previous retrospective studies. O'Neal and Robins' (1958) results may hold only for schizophrenics whose abnormal behavior brings them into contact with the criminal justice system.

In addition to O'Neal and Robins' (1958) conflicting results, methodological weaknesses apparent in the designs of the other retrospective studies discussed also serve to limit the degree of confidence that should be placed in the often-replicated finding that adult schizophrenia is related to childhood social withdrawal (Clarzio, 1968; Clarzio & McCoy, 1970). Interviewers and interviewees, for example, were generally aware both of the purposes of their interviews and of the adult psychiatric classifications of the individuals about whom information was being requested (Birren, 1944; Bowman, 1934; Frazee, 1953; Kasanin & Veo, 1932; Wittman & Steinberg, 1944). Such an open interview procedure would seem likely to produce reactive arrangements wherein interviewers' observations were recorded in terms of their expectations, and interviewees' memories were biased by their current knowledge of subjects' adult behavior (Campbell & Stanley, 1963). A second methodological weakness common to the retrospective studies is the practice of using records, made decades earlier, to check for information that was not relevant to the documents' original purposes (Birren, 1944; Bowman, 1934; Kasanin & Veo, 1932; Wittman & Steinberg, 1944). The obvious difficulty with this practice is that data on the variable of central importance, childhood social withdrawal, may not have been systematically recorded. Finally, a third methodological weakness was that investigators failed to specify precisely, in observable terms, criteria for assigning subjects to socially withdrawn and schizophrenic groups (Birren, 1944; Bowman, 1934; Kasanin & Veo, 1932; Wittman & Steinberg, 1944). These considerations, particularly in that they may have operated in interaction, represent plausible rival hypotheses for the results observed in these retrospective studies.

One final retrospective investigation reported by Bower et al. (1960) attempted to control for possible reactive arrangements. Therefore, these results represent a more methodologically sound statement of the relationship between adult schizophrenia and childhood social withdrawal. The subjects were a group of adult schizophrenics and a comparison group of a randomly selected sample of the schizophrenics' former classmates. High school records of grades and extracurricular activities and teacher interviews served as the data for the study. A double blind interview technique was followed: Neither the interviewers nor the teachers were aware of the subjects' adult psychiatric status. The teachers interviewed were told that the purpose of the study was to compare individuals' school performances with their later vocational success. Interviewers were not informed which students were schizophrenic. Consistent with the bulk of the evidence already presented, the results indicated that "with few exceptions most of the preschizophrenics could be characterized as tending toward the shut-in, withdrawing kind of personality" (Bower et al., 1960, p. 728).

Incongruent with the trend of the results thus far considered, three follow-up studies did not show social withdrawal to be a frequent precursor of adult schizophrenia. In each study, criticism is warranted because of reactive arrangements in the data-collection procedures and to the possibility of selective subject mortality and, thus, bias subject pools (Campbell & Stanley, 1963). In the first study, Morris et al. (1954) followed 54 shy, withdrawn children into adulthood. At the time of the follow-up, 37 were classified as satisfactorily adjusted, 15 as marginally adjusted but still in need of treatment, and 2 as mentally ill. Many of the subjects who achieved satisfactory adult adjustment were found to have outgoing marital partners, and spouses whose personality characteristics complemented the subjects. This factor was conjectured to compensate for subjects' shyness by bringing them into social contacts. The work experience of subjects, excluding the two who were mentally ill, was characterized as "stable," but with a tendency to hold "sheltered, protected types of jobs, in which security was a greater consideration than expanding opportunity and competition" (p. 752). In summary, many years subsequent to their initial identification, individuals termed "socially withdrawn" as children were still found to manifest discernible, although not strikingly deviant or schizophrenic, interpersonal and occupational response problems.

A second follow-up study on withdrawn children was reported by Michael et al. (1957). Their sample included 164 subjects termed "withdrawn" 14 to 29 years earlier by the Dallas Child Guidance Center. Specifically regarding the issue of association between childhood social withdrawal and adult schizophrenia, Michael et al. (1957) stated:

> The results point to the conclusion that there is not adequate justification for the assertion that children who migiht be classified as introverts are more likely to develop schizophrenia . . . or that a large proportion or schizophrenics have introverted prepsychotic personalities. [p. 337]

The results of Michael and his associates (1957) are thus consistent with those reported by Morris and his co-workers. Both follow-up studies indicated that withdrawn childhood behavior is not highly likely to lead to serious adult abnormality.

Perhaps the best-known of the follow-up studies was reported by Robins (1966). He found little distinction with respect to adult psychotic status between individuals classified as shy, fearful, and seclusive in childhood and normal controls. This finding adds further support to the contention that withdrawn children do not typically become disturbed adults.

To summarize, two types of correlational studies (retrospective and follow-up), when applied to investigate a single issue (the relationship between childhood social withdrawal and adult schizophrenia), consistently yielded contrasting results. Actually, this apparent discrepancy may be explained by the fact that each type of study investigated a separate question. The retrospective studies asked what proportion of adult schizophrenics are withdrawn as children; the follow-up studies asked what proportion of socially withdrawn children are judged schizophrenic as adults. As has been noted, methodological weaknesses limit the confidence that may be placed in the answers provided by either mode of investigation. Nevertheless, based on the evidence presently available, the answer to the first question (Were many schizophrenic adults withdrawn as children?) appears to be "yes," whereas the answer to the second question (Are many withdrawn children schizophrenic as adults?) seems to be "no."

One might posit that the extent to which childhood social withdrawal culminates in schizophrenia depends upon intervening environmental factors. Social withdrawal restricts children's access to positive social stimulation. In many cases, this situation serves to increase their likelihood of exposure to aversive social stimulation. These conditions might be contributing factors to the development of adult schizophrenic repertoires (Ferster, 1965; Patterson & Reid, 1969). Presumably, much could be done to reduce socially withdrawn children's prospects for developing adult schizophrenic repertoires if the contingencies in their environments were altered to increase their positive social contacts and limit their aversive social encounters.

Although most socially withdrawn children do not develop schizophrenic repertoires as adults, there still is a need to modify their social behavior. As noted earlier, developmental delays in a number of areas of personal and academic competency are frequently associated with low interaction levels. Children receiving restricted amounts of social stimulation from peers probably experience concomitant reductions in the physical and biological stimulation they receive (Bijou, 1966). Waiting until socially withdrawn children are "ready" to play with peers, rather than systematically arranging their environments to increase their probability of interactive behavior, may result in the forfeiture of years of vital learning opportunities.

Educational Procedures

Some (Bloom, 1964) believe that environmental manipulations have optimum impact while children are young, a time when their behavioral repertoires are undergoing rapid expansion and refinement. The most efficacious time, therefore, to influence human social development is when children are young and first learning to interact with their peers (Apolloni & Cooke, 1975). In accordance with this perspective, numerous attempts have been made to study the levels of interaction of young children while experimentally altering their environment. In this section, there is a critical review of procedures that have been purported effective for increasing Type II withdrawn children's social interaction. Evaluative research on guidance counselor procedures is presented and a cursory review of the historical development of operant conditioning tactics for controlling social interaction in outlined. Next, a critical survey of applied behavior analysis procedures for modifying isolate behavior is included, followed by a discussion of needed generalization research.

GUIDANCE COUNSELOR PROCEDURES

Educational authorities long have recognized the need to develop intervention strategies that increase the social interaction and peer acceptance of socially withdrawn children. Prior to the past decade, the strategies suggested for stimulating the social relations of withdrawn children were primarily in the form of anecdotal information about teacher attitude and practice. Baker and Traphagen (1935), for example, stated,

> To force this child to express himself or to take an active part in school is never successful. Gentle methods of praising and encouraging must be used. Any word or idea expressed by him must be recognized with extravagant interest so that he may wish to try again. Positions of honor and responsibility should be given him in order that some of his daydreams may come true. Chances for unfair competition and failure must be minimized. [p. 216]

More recently, other writers outlined guidance counselor strategies to assist socially rejected children in gaining peer acceptance (e.g., Amidon & Hoffman, 1963) and tested the efficacy of these strategies (e.g., Amidon & Hoffman, 1965; Early, 1968). The dependent variables in these studies were sociometric indices of peer acceptance or popularity. Since children who demonstrate low social-behavior rates are often the same as those who are infrequently chosen as a preferred playmate on sociogram measures (Charlesworth & Hartup, 1967; Marshall & McCandless, 1957), these studies are pertinent to a discussion of the socially withdrawn.

Recommended guidance counselor techniques included: (1) the

creation of an accepting classroom atmosphere through increased teacher acceptance of all pupils, (2) group discussions and role playing to heighten children's understanding of the feelings associated with one another's social roles, (3) awarding isolates status responsibilities in the classroom, and (4) teacher conferences directly with isolates (Amidon & Hoffman, 1963). Evaluative studies regarding the efficacy of these and similar techniques, in some cases, revealed statistically significant improvements by isolates in their classroom sociometric position (Amidon, 1961; Flanders & Havumaki, 1960; Kerstetler & Sargent, 1940; Moreno & Jennings, 1944; Northway, 1944). Individual changes, however, generally were small, and no assessments were made of the durability of the changes achieved. Furthermore, these changes typically were arranged in settings outside the classroom (Bonney, 1971) and the independent variables employed were neither specified in operational, repeatable terms, nor systematically monitored. A number of additional evaluations of these same tactics, moreover, resulted in nonsignificant changes for experimental versus control subjects (Amidon & Hoffman, 1965; Chennault, 1967; Cox, 1953; Dineen & Garry, 1956; Early, 1968; Kransler, Mayer, Dyer, & Munger, 1966; Mayer, Kransler, & Matthews, 1967).

While the efficacy of guidance counselor techniques has not been established in the literature, a number of conclusions with implications for future research seem warranted. First, Amidon (1961) demonstrated that teachers were significantly more successful at improving a rejected child's social acceptance when they related specified guidance techniques to particular acceptance problems. That is, individualized strategies, devised and implemented for particular children, were found more effective than "shotgun" approaches (i.e., techniques or varieties of techniques implemented irrespective of the specific nature of the problem). Secondly, Bonney (1971) noted that, although significant changes in group performance were rare in guidance counselor interventions, in each study, several students made exceptional gains on sociometric choices. Bonney (1971) concluded that "in future studies of this nature much more focus should be placed on individuals as opposed to concentration exclusively on group data" (p. 362). Thus, Amidon suggested tailoring strategies to meet individual needs and Bonney recommended using single-subject rather than group-research designs. Both of these suggestions are integral aspects of another line of research concerned with procedures for modifying the interactive behavior of socially withdrawn children, that is, those classroom interventions reported in the applied behavior analysis literature.

THE DEVELOPMENT OF APPLIED BEHAVIOR ANALYSIS PROCEDURES

In *The behavior of organisms,* Skinner (1938) defined a class of performance termed "operant behavior." Operants consisted of emitted responses controlled by their effects on the environment. Related to operant behavior, Skinner (1938) identified principles of conditioning (i.e., processes through which an organism's environment functions to control its behavior) and discussed these principles as they contribute to an understanding of the acquisition and maintenance of social behavior. Skinner (1953) maintained that "social behavior may be defined as the behavior of two or more people with respect to one another or in concert with respect to a common environment" (p. 297). Skinner posited that the behavior of individuals engaged in social interaction may be analyzed as stimuli that, along with other variables, control their mutual and reciprocal social performance. To illustrate his position, Skinner (1962) provided an early experimental analysis of cooperative and competitive forms of social behavior with pigeons as subjects.

In subsequent laboratory experiments, the operant paradigm was applied successfully in the analysis of human cooperative behavior (e.g., Altman, 1971; Azrin & Lindsley, 1956; Cohen, 1962; Cohen & Lindsley, 1964; Lindsley, 1966). These and other experiments (e.g., Azrin, Holz, Ulrich, & Goldiamond, 1961; Brackbill, 1958; Hopkins, 1968; Sheppard, 1959; Williams, 1959) demonstrated the development, maintenance, extinction, and reinstatement of various forms of social behavior. Thus, these researchers empirically validated the application of the operant paradigm for the predication and control of human social behavior.

Researchers' attention next turned to the development of strategies for modifying the social performance of psychotic children and adults; populations whose assessed deficits previously had proven intransigent to traditional therapeutic interventions (Eysenck, 1952; Havelkova, 1968; Levitt, 1957). In numerous laboratory studies, operant conditioning techniques were used either to develop human social stimuli as conditioned reinforcers (e.g.,

Lovaas *et al.*, 1964) or to shape and maintain social responses among psychotic children (e.g., Hewett, 1965; Hingtgen, Sanders, & Deyer, 1965; Hingtgen & Trost, 1966; Lovaas, Freitag, Nelson, & Whalen, 1967). These programs were proven successful for the establishment of at least preliminary social and language skills. A recent follow-up study indicated that these therapeutic changes endured, provided continuous programming was maintained (Lovaas, Koegel, Simmons, & Long, 1973).

Other researchers (Baer, Wolf, & Risley, 1968) sought to extend operant conditioning procedures to the modification of socially significant behaviors in naturalistic settings. Studies conducted in the experimental preschool at the University of Washington (Bijou, Peterson, Harris, Allen, & Johnson, 1969) resulted in the development of a methodology for evaluating intervention strategies with young children. This methodology served as the basis for the experimental analysis of children's social behavior in classroom environments (e.g., Galvin, Quay, & Werry, 1971; Hanley, 1970; Lipe & Jung, 1971). Generally, these studies followed an intrasubject replication design (Sidman, 1960), often referred to as the ABAB or the reversal design. In this design type, subject's behavior serves as its own control. Intrasubject replication designs are purported to allow an assessment of the degree to which a dependent variable (some index of interaction) may be altered as a function of changes in the independent variable (some aspect of the physical or social environment). Thus, reversal designs allow the determination of whether or not a functional relationship exists between an independent and a dependent variable (Baer *et al.*, 1968; Sidman, 1960).

APPLIED BEHAVIOR ANALYSIS CLASSROOM PROCEDURES

Evaluated on the basis of intrasubject replication designs, applied behavior analysis interventions have been implemented extensively in classroom settings to modify children's academic and social performance. Among these intervention tactics, a number were demonstrations of procedures for modifying social withdrawal. These strategies were attempts to make orderly changes in environmental contingencies as means of initiating and maintaining isolates' interactive behavior. The variables manipulated in these procedures may be considered in terms of four categories:

teacher attention, physical events, peer attention, and modeling. Although the tactics included in these categories all proved successful for increasing isolate children's social interaction, certain procedural difficulties were evident with each. This section critically reviews the procedures comprising these categories, and notes suggested innovations related to each.

Teacher-Attention Procedures

The results of many experimental demonstrations have indicated that teacher attention, when contingently applied to appropriate social behavior, functioned as a positive reinforcer to modify isolate performance (Allen, Hart, Buell, Harris, & Wolf, 1964; Apolloni & Cooke, 1975; Baer & Wolf, 1970; Blasdek, 1968; Cooke, Cooke, Wirtz, & Apolloni, 1974; Hall & Broden, 1967; Hart et al., 1968; Sibley et al., 1967; Strain, Shores, & Abraham, in press; Strain & Timm, 1974; Whitman et al., 1970). The purposes of these experiments were to demonstrate applications of reinforcement principles in natural settings and to ameliorate clinical problems. In each case, a treatment procedure was implemented which called for administering teacher attention to isolates, contingent on their social contacts with other children. Without exception, such demonstrations resulted in reliable increases in peer interaction.

Several difficulties have been evident in research demonstrations of teacher-attention procedures. First, such tactics were costly in terms of teachers' time and attention (e.g., Allen et al., 1964; Hart et al., 1968). Research demonstrations involving teacher-attention strategies always were conducted in settings with 5:1 or lower pupil–teacher ratios. Generally, one teacher focused attention solely on the subject for an hour or more daily. Given the 15–20:1 pupil–teacher rations found in most early-childhood classroom settings (Newbouig & Klausmeier, 1969), it is questionable whether or not teachers often will be able to attend solely to individual children for the extended time periods required to shape and maintain isolates' interactive behavior. Another difficulty with teacher-attention procedures is that they must remain in effect for numbers of days before durable results are achieved. Even after 6 to 8 days of training, these procedures, in general, have not proven successful in developing effects that were resistant to extinction upon the withdrawal of teacher attention (e.g., Allen et al., 1964).

More importantly, reinforcing events are defined by their effects on behavior (Skinner, 1938). Sometimes teacher attention will not function as a motivational variable to increase children's behavior (Levin & Simmons, 1962a,b). Thus, on occasion, it may be anticipated that teacher-attention strategies will not work at all.

Research demonstrations of teacher-attention tactics were carried out by individuals experienced in applying behavior-modification principles. Before most classroom teachers can be expected to use their attention selectively to increase isolates' interaction, some degree of prerequisite training will probably be necessary. In practice, teachers are required to discriminated the occurrence of appropriate social responses and to consequate such responses with their immediate attention. Hall and Broden (1967) note that, even with abundant professional consultation and training, initially unskilled teachers took several days to effect increases in social interaction for withdrawn children.

Yet another difficulty noted in teacher-attention studies has been that teacher attention directed solely to isolate children tends to disrupt their ongoing social activity (e.g., Allen et al., 1964). It may be that teacher attention directed to peers, as opposed to isolates, is a more effective strategy.

A final procedural difficulty associated with teacher-attention procedures, as well as with other types of procedures, has been the establishment of sufficient base-rate responding by target children. When this problem was encountered, investigators relied upon (1) shaping, a procedure in which successive approximations of the desired behavior are differentially reinforced (e.g., Allen et al., 1964; Hart et al., 1968, Hingtgen & Trost, 1966), or (2) prompting, a procedure in which modeling, instructions, and/or physical guidance are utilized to increase the opportunities for reinforcing desired behavior (e.g., Kirby & Toler, 1970; Whitman et al., 1970). As suggested before, shaping isolates' social behavior in free-field settings is expensive with respect to teachers' time and attention. Shaping requires the establishment of precise stimulus–response relationships between changes in children's social performance and teachers' attention. The amount of training necessary for teachers to successfully shape social interaction probably precludes shaping from being a useful response-building tactic in most instances (Walker & Hops, 1973).

Prompting is another strategy used to generate necessary baselines for applying reinforcement programs involving teacher attention. Typically, prompting has involved an antecedent arrangement where withdrawn children and/or one or more of their peers were instructed to participate in some form of interaction. Interactions between children in prompted situations generally were not either precisely specified or systematically controlled. Such unstructured prompting between isolates and their peers may result in unwanted outcomes. Prompted interactions may produce at least four types of response sequences: positive initiations with positive responses, positive initiations with negative responses, negative initiations with negative responses, and negative initiations with positive responses. The last three of these response sequences would seem antithetical to the purposes of interventions with withdrawn children. The solution to this problem lies in greater specificity of prompted responses and the systematic fading of prompts (Kale et al., 1968).

One way to circumvent the possible liabilities associated with prompting strategies is to structure them so as to ensure high levels of prosocial responding by both targets and peers. For example, Whitman et al. (1970) described two highly structured prompting arrangements. Social responses were defined as "one child's behavior becoming mutually or reciprocally involved with a second child's behavior" (Whitman et al., 1970, p. 134). In one activity, severely retarded subjects were seated on the floor, 3 feet apart, and instructed to roll a ball back and forth to one another. In the second, they were positioned adjacent to one another and instructed to pass a block between them. Responses were initially hand shaped by two undergraduate experimenters. After both subjects completed a response, each was praised and given an M&M candy. Two additional subjects eventually were brought into the daily training sessions, one subject into each activity. The subjects whom Whitman et al. (1970) trained were Type I socially withdrawn children (see page 98). There is no reason, however, why similar procedures could not be employed with Type II children.

With Type II withdrawn children, it would seem advisable that prompting activities might include naturally occurring activities that invite interactions. Teaching dancing might be one relatively direct and natural way to prompt social interaction. Stereotyped interlocking responses are executed in dancing which facilitate the development of imitative behavior and increase isolates' rates of social responding in the presence of peer stimuli. Moreover, aside from applying teachers' attention, music is a reinforcer (Wilson & Hopkins, 1973) inherent in dancing which is readily amenable to contingent application by teachers. Making music to peer groups contingent on the participation of isolate children might be one way to assure the latter's involvement.

A second suggestion regarding how more naturally to prompt children's interactions might be termed "buddying." Morris et al. (1954) reported that many of the withdrawn children they followed, who later achieved satisfactory adult adjustment, had outgoing marital partners. The spouses were said to have increased the subjects' social responsiveness through interacting with them and through bringing them into social contacts with others. A related, potentially fruitful tactic that teachers could pursue is to pair withdrawn children with a buddy who would attempt to integrate them into peer groups. Teacher attention or some other reinforcing event could be supplied to the buddy contingent on increased levels of social interaction by isolates.

In summary, procedures relying on teacher attention were found highly reliable for increasing isolates' interactive behavior with their peers. Numerous procedural difficulties, however, are associated with applying teacher-attention modification programs. These difficulties together with a number of tactical suggestions, were discussed.

Physical-Event Procedures

Physical attributes of classroom environments represent another category of variables that influence children's levels of peer interaction. In particular, two properties of the physical arrangement of environments have been manipulated systematically with resulting changes in social behavior: (1) the arrangement of objects in space (Johnson, 1935; Sommer & Ross, 1958), and (2) the play pattern, "isolate" or "social" associated with available objects (e.g., Parten, 1933; Quilitch & Risley, 1973).

The literature bearing on the first of these attributes has contributed only indirectly to teaching procedures for increasing interaction. Very little is known about the effects of the arrangement of objects in space on children's social behavior. However, there was reported some research that suggests that particular arrangements of physical events in environmental settings bear some relationship to the occurrence of interaction among inhabitants. Sommer and Ross (1958), for example, manipulated furniture arrangements on geriatric wards and noted correlated increases in social interactions. A similar correlation may exist in classroom environments. Johnson (1935) reported increased frequencies of social contacts between classmates as a function of reducing the amount of available playground equipment. Teachers attempting to modify isolates' behavior might consider altering the arrangement of objects in their classrooms to promote interaction between children.

A second attribute of physical events in classrooms, the usage pattern associated with available materials, also was shown to be related to levels of social interactions among children. As early as 1933, Parten reported normative data on the degree of social participation demonstrated by children involved in play activities with various toys. At least 60 observations were made of 34 subjects, 2 to 4 years old, for 1 minute each. Parten found that house and doll play were the activities associated with the highest incidence of observed social interaction. Characteristically, sand play and constructive work with clay, paper, beads, and paint were found to be nonsocial play activities.

In a more recent investigation, Quilitch and Risley (1973) functionally analyzed the effects of various play materials on children's social behavior. Based on prebaseline observations of children's play, the investigators identified two types of toys. One type (isolate toys) usually was used by one child; the second type (social toys) often was played with simultaneously by two or more children. They divided 24 subjects into 4 6-member groups. Each group was presented 3 examples of a toy type (either isolate or social) for 15 minutes. Next, the toys were removed and the groups were supplied with the alternate toy type, again for 15 minutes. The dependent variables of interest were percentage of time in play with materials and percentage of time spent playing with other children. Results indicated that the subjects spent a large percentage of time in play under both conditions (96% with isolate toys and 98% with social toys), but that the type of play, social or isolate, varied dramatically as a function of the type of toy being used. The same results were apparent in a second experiment involving an across-days intrasubject replication design. The investigators concluded that

> the study of the effects of toys upon children's social behaviors allows the applied psychologist to create developmental or therapeutic play environments that promote social behaviors previously found amenable only to individual remediation programs. [Quilitch & Risley, 1973, p. 578].

The assertion that toys may be of therapeutic value was lent additional support in a number of procedural demonstrations. In each instance, an increase in social interaction was effected after training withdrawn children in the correct use of toys which required motor and social skills. Buell, Stoddard, Harris, and Baer (1968) socially reinforced a 3-year-old female isolate for using outdoor play equipment in an indirect attempt to increase her level of social interaction with peers. Following a baseline stage, the teacher initiated a priming activity in which the child was placed and held on a piece of outdoor play equipment for 30 seconds each day. Thereafter, the teacher attended to the child while she remained on the equipment. Increases were noted both in the child's use of the equipment and in her level of peer interaction. Similar results were reported by Johnston, Kelly, Harris, and Wolf (1966). These authors increased a withdrawn boy's level of social interaction by socially reinforcing climbing responses, particularly climbing responses on a jungle gym.

Allen, Turner, and Everett (1970) also presented a behavioral investigation that indicated the influence that training isolate children to use play materials may have on their social behavior. The study involved a 4-year-old boy. Deciding that it would be unproductive to try to establish cooperative play behavior until he first developed some individual play skills, his teachers instituted a step-by-step program to teach the child to play appropriately with several materials found in the classroom. Next, the child was reinforced for using the play materials with other children. By the end of the study, the child spent 70% of his free-play time engaged in cooperative play.

Another way to use material events to increase isolates' play with peers was presented by Kirby and Toler (1970). These investigators induced a 5-year-old boy to pass out choices of candy to his peers just before free-play periods. Once the procedure was instituted, the child increased his level of peer interaction in free play. One of the interpretations of this finding was that the withdrawn subject increased his reinforcement value to his peers through being paired with candy (Kirby & Toler, 1970). If this interpretation is correct, it also might hold that other events more natural to the classroom setting could be paired with isolates to facilitate peer interaction. Withdrawn subjects could be allowed open access to prized play materials provided that they use them with other children. This tactic could involve first training isolates to play appropriately with valued materials and then allowing other children to use the materials only so long as isolates were included. Presumably, these tactics would increase isolates' reinforcement value to their peers and thereby increase the rate at which peers interact with them.

In conclusion, two physical attributes of classroom environments were shown to have at least correlational relationships to children's social behavior: the arrangement of objects in space and the social value of available materials. Training isolates to use play materials resulted in increases in their interaction levels. The literature provided a basis for suggesting that it may be of value to establish associations between withdrawn children and highly reinforcing materials.

Peer-Attention Procedures

Several experimenters have investigated the influence of peer reinforcement on levels of social responsiveness. Wahler (1967), for example, demonstrated that the social behavior of preschoolers in free field settings is subject to the reinforcement control of peer attention. Moreover, Wahler (1967) reported that children may control one another's behavior in accordance with an experimenter's instructions. This control, however, was maintained for only 5-minute periods. Presumably, therapeutic interventions would require longer periods of contingent peer attention.

Other researchers sought arrangements that would ensure more sustained periods of peer reinforcement contingent on the social performance of withdrawn children. Walker and Hops (1973) evaluated the effects of four different contingency arrangements for inducing interaction between first- and second-grade withdrawn subjects and their peers. For each contingency arrangement, a withdrawn subject and/or her peers were reinforced for the others' initiated responses. In all, three experiments were carried out, each in a separate classroom. In each experiment, the subject and/ or her peers first viewed and discussed an observational training film (O'Connor, 1969; 1972) designed to teach withdrawn children social skills while reducing their avoidance reactions to peers. Instructions to the subjects and/or peers regarding the contingencies for the various experiments were issued immediately following the training film. The number of points earned was announced at the end of each session and was recorded on charts located in the classrooms.

Experimental training conditions were in effect for a total of 30 minutes each school day in each classroom. In Experiment I, the target subject earned points toward self-selected backup reinforcers when peers initiated social responses to her. In Experiment II, two contingency arrangements were put into effect. During condition one, peers viewed the observational training film and were provided with a group-selected reward contingent upon the target subject's social initiations to them. The subject was not informed about the group contingency in effect, until intervention condition two. At that time (the third contingency arrangement) both the subject and her peers could earn rewards for the subject's initiated social responses.

In the final experiment, Walker and Hops (1973) established a fourth arrangement described as a "double interlocking reinforcing contingency" (p. 294). Under this arrangement, peers earned a group consequence when the subject initiated 25 social responses, and the subject earned an individual consequence when her peers initiated 75 social responses. Both response requirements had to be met before either the subject or her peers could receive reinforcement.

The results from the three experiments (evaluated on the basis of reversal designs) revealed that all four contingency arrangements produced increased rates of social interaction by subjects. Furthermore, in each case, reciprocity characterized the changes in the response levels between the subjects and their peers. Increases and decreases in levels of social interaction initiated by isolates and peers tended to co-vary across the various conditions studied.

Moreover, the second contingency arrangement in Experiment II was found associated with greater effects than the first. In this arrangement, the subject was both aware of the contingencies and allowed to share in the group consequence earned through her initiations to peers. The double interlocking contingency used in Experiment III resulted in the most dramatic and consistent social-performance increases for a withdrawn subject. No data were reported on the children's social responding at times other than when training was in effect.

Another way to increase isolates' interactions by using tokens and a group contingency may be to dispense tokens straightforwardly to subjects and their peers contingent on differential response changes involving both (Kazdin, 1971). Numerous response sequences could be structured theoretically. For example, isolates could be issued tokens by peers for initiating social interactions, whereas peers could be issued tokens by isolates for attention to isolates' social initiations. One suggested way to implement such a tactic will be discussed in the next subsection of this chapter, which reviews modeling procedures.

One of the simplest and most direct ways to increase withdrawn children's peer interactions may be to structure opportunities for them to interact with peers younger than themselves. Suomi and Harlow (1972) and Gomber and Mitchell (1974) reported therapeutic interventions with noninteractive primates. Working with 6-month-old isolate-reared monkeys, a subject population whose behavioral abnormalities previously had appeared unalterable, the investigators were successful in developing social repertoires in isolates which made them indistinguishable from their normal peers. This occurred after the isolate-reared monkeys were exposed daily over a 6- or 7-month period to socially normal monkeys 3 or more months younger than themselves. While caution must be exercised in generalizing these findings to human subjects (Harlow, Gluck, & Suomi, 1972), the effects achieved by Suomi and Harlow (1972) and by Gomber and Mitchell (1974) lend some support to the idea of restructuring class groupings across ages as an intervention tactic with isolates.

Two studies have been reported which investigated the effects of restructuring groups on human social behavior. Hauserman, Walen, and Behling (1973) restructured seating arrangements as a procedure to socially integrate five black children into an otherwise all-white classroom. The authors provided social and tangible reinforcers for cross-racial seating during lunchtime to stimulate contacts between white and black children. The procedure resulted in increased cross-racial interaction by black and white children during a free-play period following lunch. Similarly, Levison (1971) used daily periods of dramatic play with peers who issued high levels of attention to playmates to increase social participation by isolates.

The nature of the activity included in structured play situations is probably of utmost importance. Tasks that require cooperation seem to be effective in promoting prosocial interactions among young children. Stendler, Damrin, and Haines (1951) observed the free-play social behavior of 7-year-old children following their participation in either cooperative or competitive work sessions. The occurrence of friendly conversations, sharing, and helping were found highest following cooperative training sessions. Additionally, based on sociometric data, Kinney (1953) achieved reductions in the number of isolates and rejected children by teaching in small cooperating groups, as opposed to either instructing the class by ability groups or as a whole. Finally, Altman (1971) found increases in the cooperative behavior of children during a free-play period after their participation in a simple cooperative laboratory training exercise. Each study suggested a relationship between cooperative activities and increased interpersonal involvement between children. Research to determine whether or not this same relationship holds for isolate children seems warranted.

To summarize, peer attention is a stimulus event having demonstrated reinforcement value (Wahler, 1967). The major difficulty in using peer attention to modify isolates' social behaviors has been the problem of maintaining control over peer attention. Group contingency procedures have produced reliable increases in training (Walker & Hops, 1973), but have not, as yet, been shown to result in generalized performance increases under nontraining conditions. Work by Suomi and Harlow (1972) and by Gomber and Mitchel (1974) suggested there may be some benefit to allowing isolates numerous opportunities to interact with younger peers. Similarly, studies with humans have shown that restructuring classroom activity groups has led to increased social interaction for isolates (Hauserman et al., 1973; Levison, 1971). Finally, among normal groups of children, increased prosocial responding has been noted in play sessions following cooperative activities (Altman, 1971; Kinney, 1953; Stendler et al., 1951). It has been suggested that this same relation may hold for isolate children.

Modeling Procedures

Modeling is another way in which peers and teachers have assisted in modifying isolates' behavior. Bandura (1969) noted that modeling is a most effective therapeutic strategy for social behavior because most social responses are acquired naturally through imitation. Bandura and Walters (1963) defined imitation as behavior demonstrated by a subject which is similar to that of a model previously observed. Their definition specified a stimulus–response relationship with little consideration of the roles played by rehearsal or consequent stimuli. This conceptualization of imitation was employed as an inderpinning framework for a variety of therapeutic behavioral interventions (e.g., Bandura, Grusec, & Menlove, 1967; Bandura & Menlove, 1968). The term "observational training" used in this volume refers to imitative behavior generated by therapeutic procedures based on the Bandura and Walters' (1963) paradigm. Observational training does not dictate that an imitative response be made by the observer for learning to occur. Moreover, if an observer's response does occur, the observational training paradigm does not require that the response be consequated. In short, observational training requires only that an observer view a model.

According to Bandura and Walters (1963), three effects accrue from observational training. First, modeling effects occur when observers emit novel responses following demonstrations by models. Secondly, observational learning produces inhibiting and disinhibiting effects. By this it is meant that observers emit or fail to emit modeled responses already in their repertoires as a result of their observations of response consequences to models. Thirdly, observational learning has eliciting effects. Eliciting effects occur when observers exhibit previously learned responses following their demonstration by models who do not receive response consequences for their performances. All three of these effects have been held to account for increases in social performance by withdrawn children following their exposure to observational training procedures.

In an application of observational training, O'Connor (1969, 1972) used film-mediated models to increase occurrences of peer interaction by socially withdrawn children. In one study, O'Connor (1969) selected 13 (6 experimental and 7 control) preschool isolate subjects on the basis of teacher referrals and objective behavioral observations. The data consisted of pre- and posttraining observations of isolate children during free play in their regular classroom settings. Each observation included 32 3-second intervals. "A social interaction was defined as any behavior directed toward another child which involved a reciprocal quality" (O'Connor, 1969, p. 17).

Following the collection of pretest data, both experimental and control subjects viewed 20-minute sound–color films. The movie seen by the experimental subjects portrayed 11 scenes in which a model child was shown, first observing the social interactions of peers, and then joining in their interaction with pleasant consequences. A narrator directed isolate viewers' attention to relevant cues in the film. Control subjects viewed a film with no human characters accompanied by a musical soundtrack.

Posttest data on both groups were collected in a single session immediately upon returning to their classroom. The six children who viewed the observational training film significantly increased their pre- to posttest level of social interaction ($t = 2.29$; $p < 0.03$). Compared with the control subjects, the observation-trained subjects' change score was significantly greater ($t = 2.53$; $p < 0.01$), as was their level of social interaction at the time of the posttest observation ($t = 2.70$; $p < 0.01$). Within-group comparisons of the control subjects reflected no statistically significant differences in that group. Close examination of the trained children's prefilm and postfilm levels of social interaction made it evident that most of the group's change score was attributable to marked increases made by only two subjects. Although all experimental subjects increased their level of social interaction following training, two of them (the two lowest prior to treatment) still would have been classified as "isolates" according to O'Connor's (1969) selection criteria. Based on grouped data, then, the application of O'Connor's procedure was shown to be correlated with increased social performance. The data on individual subjects, however, revealed that group gains noted in social interaction were not representative of all the subjects in the treatment group. Viewing the results on the basis of individual performance, one is hard-pressed to accept O'Connor's (1969) assessment that "the present results established symbolic modeling as a highly efficacious procedure for modifying social withdrawal" (p. 19).

In a systematic replication of his 1969 study, O'Connor (1972) investigated the comparative effects of observational training and shaping on the social interactions of isolate nursery school children. The 31 isolate subjects were assigned to 1 of 4 group conditions: observational training (OT), $N = 9$; observational training and shaping (OT + S), $N = 7$; shaping (S), $N = 8$; and control (C), $N = 7$. The subjects in the OT and OT + S groups viewed an observational training film while the subjects in the S and C groups viewed a control film. Following the viewings, each of the subjects in the OT + S and S groups received "5 hr. of praise and attention spread over a 2-weak period" (p. 329). In this shaping exercise, a trained graduate student dispensed his attention contingent on subject interactions. Data were collected at four separate sessions on each subject. Prefilm observations were recorded 1 to 4 weeks prior to viewing the film; postfilm observations were collected immediately following viewing sessions. Two follow-up observations were recorded at 3 and 6 weeks following the postfilm sessions.

O'Connor's (1972) results replicated his 1969 findings: Subjects receiving observational training (OT and OT + S) were significantly more likely to interact following treatment than untrained (S and C) subjects ($t = 2.81$, $p < .005$). Related to the effects of shaping, O'Connor (1972) found that (1) S subjects increased significantly more than C subjects ($t = 2.56$, $p < .01$) but that (2) OT + S subjects increased no more than OT subjects ($t = .25$, $p > .4$). This finding suggests that shaping did not add to the effects of observational training. A comparison between S and OT + S groups revealed no significant differences ($t = 30$, $p > .25$) in levels of social interaction while shaping was in effect; but when shaping was discontinued, the level of interaction for S subjects was significantly lower than that of OT + S subjects ($t = 2.94$, $p < .005$). These results indicated that shaping was effective but that its effects were limited to the period soon after shaping was applied.

Because of the manner in which the study was conducted, and the incompleteness of the data reported, O'Connor's (1972) findings should be interpreted cautiously. As reported, shaping consisted of only 5 hours of treatment spread haphazardly across a 2-week period. No record of the shaper's behavior was maintained. This makes it impossible to determine the manner in which the shaping was conducted. Moreover, O'Connor (1969) failed to report the performance of individual subjects. This omission makes it impossible to determine the extent to which the averages for the various groups studied were representative of the interaction levels demonstrated by individual subjects.

Based on individual data reported for the six experimental subjects in the 1969 study, it seems reasonable to generalize that O'Connor's observational training procedure would be clinically successful (as judged immediately subsequent to treatment) with about two-thirds of treated children. Moreover, based on this limited data, it appears that O'Connor's procedure is least successful with children who demonstrate extremely low baseline rates of interaction. The likelihood that this, in fact, is the case was given support by the results of a recent study by Walker and Hops (1973).

On the basis of teacher reports on the classroom behavior of 1067 first-, second-, and third-grade children, Walker and Hops (1973) selected the 12 children rated most withdrawn and observed their free-play behavior. From this group, the three children who demonstrated the lowest observed rates of social interaction were selected as subjects for the various contingency arrangements evaluated in the study. This selection criteria ensured the identification of target subjects who demonstrated extremely low rates of peer interaction. Once selected, two of the withdrawn subjects were shown the O'Connor (1969) film and then exposed to a contingency arrangement designed to effect their levels of interaction. (In Experiment III, the peer group but not the subject was shown the film.) Unfortunately, the designs for these two experiments did not include component analyses of the observational training procedure's contribution toward the results obtained. Two findings, however, suggested that the independent effects of observational training were minimal. First, no immediate increase in social responding was noted on the part of either subject immediately after viewing the observational training film. Secondly, the social performance of the isolate subjects who viewed the observational training film returned to near baseline levels as soon as the reinforcement programs were withdrawn. These findings indicate that O'Connor's (1969) observational training procedure is unlikely to produce therapeutic outcomes with children who demonstrate extremely low levels of peer interaction.

Observational training is probably an intervention tactic of limited value in teaching adaptive social repertoires to severely withdrawn children. First, a history of reinforcement for imitative behavior is probably a prerequisite for satisfactory outcomes. Many socially withdrawn children lack this history, particularly Type I children. Furthermore, as Bandura (1966) noted, observational learning operates in the determination of those responses that will be "tried," not those that will become characteristic aspects of the observers' repertoire. The latter condition, it would seem, is much more a result of the consequences of the observers' behaviors once responses are "tried," that is, the reinforcers or punishers produced. Consistent with this position, Bandura et al. (1967) recommended the combined use of observational training and reinforcement procedures in behavior therapy. This arrangement constitutes what is herein termed "imitation training," a modeling procedure based on an operant learning-theory foundation.

Skinner (1953) defined imitation as a stimulus–response–stimulus relationship, which occurs when the behavior of one person servers as a discriminative stimulus controlling the matching behavior of another person. The discriminative properties of the antecedent stimulus are established as a result of its presence at the time a particular response is reinforced. Since it sets the occasion for the reinforcement of the response, models' behaviors serve to increase the probability of matching responses by observers.

A number of investigators (e.g., Baer, Peterson, & Sherman, 1967; Lovaas, Berberich, Perloff, & Schaeffer, 1966; Paloutzian, Hasazi, Steifel, & Edgar, 1971) have reported the successful use of imitation training procedures to increase the occurrence of social responses by Type I socially withdrawn children. Imitation training, however, has not been employed to increase social interaction among Type II children in classroom settings. Doing so would offer several advantages over the observational training procedure currently advocated (O'Connor, 1969, 1972). First, imitation training provides the mechanism necessary for structuring mutually reinforcing interaction, characterized by anxiety reduction, between isolates and peers. Secondly, as noted previously, imitation training operates to determine responses maintained, not just those "tried" (Bandura, 1966). Imitation training ensures that initial social responses by isolates will be strengthened. Finally, imitation training, although not as it has been typically used, could be structured to produce differential response changes by subjects and their classmates. Isolates could be taught to initiate themselves into peer activities, to invite others to join in their activities, and to maintain interactions once they are begun. Peers could be instructed to increase their rates of positive responses and decrease their rates of negative social responses toward isolates. Such conditions likely would result in the acquisition of more extensive social repertoires by isolates, as well as a reduction in their avoidance responses to peers.

One way to structure imitation training with Type II withdrawn children might involve combining instructions, imitation training, and role playing or rehearsal (Gittelman, 1965). Isolate children and their peers could be instructed to observe teachers as they act out brief skits with participating peers. Isolates then could be reinforced for role-playing actions modeled by teachers. Instructions to participating peers could specify that their social responses to isolates' imitations are to be positive (i.e., friendly vocal, gestural, and sharing responses). Reinforcers could be issued to isolates and peers individually or in accordance with group contingency arrangements. Individual or group tokens might be made contingent upon appropriate isolate–peer social interaction.

Role playing has long been recommended as a procedure for modifying inappropriate interpersonal behavior (S. L. Moreno, 1946; Z. T. Moreno 1965). One of the benefits attributed to role playing is that it provides children with opportunities to learn adaptive responses in fear-provoking situations (Holmes, 1936; Lazarus, 1960; S. L. Moreno, 1959; Rhodes, 1962; Wolpe, Salter, & Renya, 1965). Combining role playing with imitation training might hasten the extinction of avoidance responses to peers and further the expansion of isolates' social repertoires.

In summary, two learning-theory paradigms advanced to account for the phenomenon of imitation (Bandura & Walters, 1963; Skinner, 1953) have served as the bases for therapeutic interventions with withdrawn children (O'Connor, 1969, 1972; Paloutzian et al., 1971). O'Connor's (1969) observational training procedure proved effective in about two-thirds of cases, but ineffective when used with extremely isolated children (O'Connor, 1969; Walker & Hops,

1973). Demonstrations of imitation training procedures, on the other hand, were found highly effective with severely withdrawn (Type I) children but were not used in interventions to modify the behavior of Type II children. A training procedure that combines instructions, imitation training, and role playing was suggested as a way to apply imitation training with Type II withdrawn children.

SUMMARY OF RESEARCH ON SOCIAL WITHDRAWAL

This section has summarized psychological and educational literature establishing the significance of the problem of childhood social withdrawal. Moreover, it critically reviewed empirical and systematic teaching procedures for modifying withdrawn behavior.

"Social withdrawal" is a descriptive term applied to individuals who exhibit social behavior considered deficient by social agents controlling the reinforcers available in the environment. Socially withdrawn children exhibit low rates of social interaction with peers (Kale et al., 1968) and often are considered deviant (Gilbert, 1957; Heinstein, 1969; Rogers et al., 1955; Woody, 1964). Two levels of social withdrawal may be distinguished: Type I, repertoire deficiencies; and Type II, performance deficits.

Theoretical and empirical support was advanced for the position that social withdrawal is a response pattern frequently associated with developmental delays (e.g., Amidon & Hoffman, 1965; Ausubel, 1958; Bonney, 1971; Buswell, 1953; Hartup, 1970; Rardin & Moan, 1971; Whitman et al., 1970). Retrospective investigations of the early behavior of adult psychotics consistently revealed that social withdrawal frequently was noted in their case histories (Birren, 1944; Bower et al., 1960; Bowman, 1934; Frazee, 1953; Kasanin & Veo, 1932; Wittman & Steinberg, 1944). In contrast, three follow-up studies investigating the adult behavior of isolate children did not show social withdrawal to be a frequent precursor of adult schizophrenia (Michael et al., 1957; Morris et al., 1954; Robins, 1966). This apparent inconsistency in reported findings might be accounted for by examining the intervening environments to which withdrawn individuals are exposed in the course of their development (Ferster, 1965; Patterson & Reid, 1969). Since behavior is a product of interaction history between person and environment (Skinner, 1953), given favorable environmental circumstances, withdrawn individuals will not appear atypical as adults. However, waiting until socially withdrawn children are "ready" to play, rather than systematically arranging their environments to increase the probability of their interactive behavior, may result in forfeiting years of vital learning opportunities (Apolloni & Cooke, 1975).

Guidance counseling procedures for modifying social withdrawal were not generally successful (e.g., Amidon & Hoffman, 1965; Chennault, 1967; Early, 1968). Two developers of guidance counselor strategies (Amidon, 1961; Bonney, 1971) proposed methodological revisions congruent with standard practices in applied behavioral research.

Teacher attention has been used as a reinforcer to modify social withdrawal (e.g., Sibley et al., 1967). Difficulties associated with implementing teacher attention procedures limit their widespread applicability (Walker & Hops, 1973). A number of suggestions were made regarding ways to circumvent procedural difficulties associated with teacher-attention procedures.

Physical events present in classroom environments were discussed as another category of variables amenable for manipulation to modify social withdrawal. Play pattern ("isolate" or "social") generally associated with various play materials was found to be highly associated with children's levels of social interactions (Parten, 1933; Quilitch & Risley, 1973). Training withdrawn children to use play materials appropriately proved to be an effective means for stimulating their social relationships with peers (Allen et al., 1970; Buell et al., 1968; Johnston et al., 1966). It was suggested that the social reinforcing value of isolates may be bolstered by training isolates to play with popular materials and then allowing other children to use these materials only so long as isolates were included.

Peer attention also was described as a variable that may be utilized to effect isolates' social behavior. Programs utilizing group contingencies proved effective for establishing sustained periods of peer reinforcement contingent on withdrawn children's social performance (Walker & Hops, 1973). Work by primate ethologists (Gomber & Mitchell, 1974; Suomi & Harlow, 1972) with isolates suggested that structuring situations that induce isolates to interact with peers younger than themselves may be one of the simplest and most naturally direct ways to modify their behavior. Tasks that require children to cooperate with one another aid in promoting prosocial interaction among young normal children (Altman, 1971; Kinney, 1953; Stendler *et al.*, 1951). Cooperation training also may be a method by which to increase interaction between isolates and peers.

A fourth category of procedures for modifying isolate behavior has been modeling tactics. These procedures were used to establish imitative social behavior. Imitation was defined from two theoretical perspectives. Bandura and Walters (1963) defined it as behavior demonstrated by a subject which is similar to that of a model previously observed. Their definition specified a stimulus–response relationship with little consideration of the roles played by learner's rehearsals, or the stimuli that consequate them, in response acquisition situations. Skinner (1953), as distinct from Bandura and Walters, maintained that imitation involves a stimulus–response–stimulus relationship. In Skinner's formulation, the model's behavior serves as a discriminative stimuli (i.e., a controlling antecedent stimuli event) that operates to control the probability of the imitative response of an observer. Whether the imitative response will occur depends upon past reinforcement to the observer for matching behavior.

O'Connor (1969; 1972) demonstrated an observational training procedure for modifying social withdrawal. This procedure was found successful in about two-thirds of cases but appeared least successful with children who exhibited extremely low baseline rates of interaction (O'Connor, 1969, 1972; Walker & Hops, 1973). Numerous investigations were reported in which imitation training was used with Type I socially withdrawn children (e.g., Paloutzian *et al.*, 1971), but none were reported which dealt with Type II withdrawn children in classroom settings. An imitation training procedure that combines instructions, imitation training, and role playing was suggested and described for use with Type II socially withdrawn children.

The Issue of Generalization

One major criticism of these behavior modification procedures for treating maladaptive prosocial interaction concerns the paucity of instances in which the issue of generalization from training has been assessed empirically. Generalization is an important consideration in devising any behavior-change program. Transfer of training to other settings and spread of training effects to nonconditioned responses should be integral considerations in all behavior modification efforts. It seems likely that procedures to facilitate prosocial responding could be considerably improved if researchers systematically investigated the variables responsible for obtaining generalized changes in performance.

Although the issue of generalization does not seem to have received as much professional attention as its significance would warrant, it has not been totally ignored (Griffith & Craighead, 1972; Kazdin & Craighead, 1973; Terrace, 1966). Reynolds (1967) defined the phenomenon of generalization as the extent to which behavioral-rate increases noted under one set of conditions occur concomitantly in other stimulus situations. Terrace (1966) advocated that the term "generalization" be eliminated from the applied behavior analysis terminology and replaced with the term "stimulus control." Terrace (1966) argued that this replacement is warranted since generalization is a descriptive construct while stimulus control refers to an empirical function. Mowrer (1971), in referring to the same behavioral phenomenon (generalization), used the term "transfer of training." Regardless of the term applied—generalization, stimulus control, or transfer of training—the phenomena of interest are the extent to which a behavior trained in one environment is exhibited in another environment and/or the extent to which response covariations occur among nontrained responses.

Generalization has been referred to by differing terms and discussed from varying perspectives; nevertheless, its significance, and, in fact, crucial importance in determining the success of behavioral treatment programs, is recognized across perspectives and orientations (Carpenter, 1974; Willems, 1974). For the purposes of the present chapter, generalization will be considered in terms of its two dominant subdivisions: stimulus generalization and response generalization. Stimulus generalization is a generic term applied to situations wherein a response is emitted in the presence of a stimulus other than the one it was originally conditioned to follow. Stimulus generalization subsumes transfer of training across settings, across individuals, and over time. Response generalization occurs when collateral response changes are noted in a training environment or in another environmental setting outside of training (i.e., in a setting generalization situation).

PROGRAMMING FOR GENERALIZED OUTCOMES

Applied behavior analysis is a relatively young discipline. Over the past two decades, a great deal of effort has been expended to demonstrate that a variety of areas in human performance may be brought under environmental control. As a consequence of this work, the tenets and principles of behavior analysis and environmental engineering are now widely accepted as applicable for modifying many forms of human activity (Carpenter, 1974; Skinner, 1974). Applied behavior analysis must necessarily be directed toward programming for the elusive phenomena of generalization. Having demonstrated control over human behavior in laboratory and applied settings, behavior analysts must now plan for more global, less circumscribed, therapeutic outcomes from their treatments; that is, they must investigate ways to program for generalization. One direct course of action to advance scientific understanding and pragmatic application in the area of generalization would be to intensify efforts to analyze and program generalized effects from behavioral interventions. Some researchers (e.g., Kale et al., 1968; Kazdin & Polster, 1973) have begun this most important work, but much remains to be accomplished. One long identified (Miller & Dollard, 1941; Osgood, 1949; Thorndike, 1949; Skinner, 1938) and empirically validated (Terrace, 1966) conclusion is that generalized effects from training can be expected to occur to the extent that components of the training situation and generalization situation are similar. That is, the more similar other environments are to the training environment, the more generalized effects should be expected (other variables held constant). This principle is perhaps the major factor responsible for the trend in the behavior modification movement to conduct treatment programs in natural environments (i.e., settings wherein behavers spend most of their time) (Tharp & Wetzel, 1969). Many considerations, however, mitigate against the implementation of behavioral interventions in natural environments (Repucci & Saunders, 1974). Frequently, the environmental control necessary to effect therapeutic behavior change cannot be gained. Working under this realistic limitation, teaching procedures must be developed which maximize the probability that, once behavers acquire socially significant responses, their responses maintain in settings outside of training. One well-documented conclusion is that, if interventions cannot be successfully implemented in natural settings, programmers should plan the training environment so as to make it as similar as possible to the natural environment of the consumer (Lent, 1968; Reppucci & Saunders, 1974).

Another widely accepted conclusion evident from research regarding the generalized effects of behavioral interventions is that generalization cannot be expected reliably to occur in the absence of programming specifically designed to attain it (Garcia & De-Haven, 1974; Hanley, 1970; Kazdin & Craighead, 1973). Research that included probes for generalized treatment effects, without intervention tactics to maximize such effects, almost uniformly found no generalization (e.g., O'Leary & Drabman, 1971; Sailor, 1971). Other research, however, that included intervention strategies specifically designed to produce setting and response generalization has shown that these phenomena can be experimentally induced (Kale et al., 1968; Kazdin & Polster, 1973; McLean & Raymore, 1972; Walker & Buckley, 1972).

Three types of strategies for programming generalization have been reported in the professional literature. First, it has been shown that overconditioning (Jackson, Stanex, Lane & Dominguez, 1938) can be used as an effective tool to maximize generalization. Overconditioning has been conceptualized as a tactic wherein responses are conditioned to such an extent in the training situation that they also come to be demonstrated outside of training. Baer and Wolf (1970), for example, provided an example of generalization across time brought about through an overconditioning paradigm. These investigators alternately applied and withdrew a conditioning package consisting of priming and teacher attention. The intervention resulted in social-behavior change by a preschool child which eventually maintained in the absence of the training procedure. Similarly, Cooke (1974) successfully used overconditioning to program for generalization from training designed to increase social–emotional behaviors by elementary-age learning-disabled children. Cooke used a direct teaching procedure consisting of instructions, modeling, and social consequation over an extended period of time until generalization across settings was noted. Moreover, integrating trained subjects with naive class-mates in a free-play setting, Cooke demonstrated that reciprocal changes in certain social–emotional response indices were evidenced by naive subjects. Probes to assess generalization across time indicated that the positive social–emotional response increases effected for both trained and naive subjects endured for 4 weeks (the period of time from the termination of training to the end of the school year when data collection was terminated necessarily).

Other investigators have reported control of a range of diverse responses following the utilization of specific training tactics to increase a limited number of response events. Baer and Sherman (1964), Lovaas et al. (1966), and Brigham and Sherman (1968) noted response generalization in training settings following extended imitation training. Whitman et al. (1970) noted stimulus and response generalization following continued training (two daily sessions for 6 weeks) wherein severely mentally retarded subjects were taught to share materials with peers. Trained subjects demonstrated increases in their social responding toward trained and untrained peers in another setting following training. Response generalization to the second situation also was evident in that the subjects increased their social participation for activities other than those directly trained.

Another mode of programming generalization has involved training in natural environments as well as in structured training environments. There is evidence to indicate that adaptive behaviors are more likely to occur in natural environments after they have been reinforced in several structured training environments (Garcia, 1974; Griffith & Craighead, 1972; Lent, 1968; Lyon, 1971). Lyon (1971), for example, programmed generalization across setting for the question-answering behavior of schizophrenics. He reported that the subject answered questions in an untrained setting only after such behavior had been reinforced in several training environments. Likewise, Garcia (1974) programmed across settings and trainers to teach a generalized conversational speech form to retarded children. Training effects were noted in a generalization setting only after successful training had been completed in two training settings. Garcia also included probes for untrained responses to a setting outside the original training situation. Initially, no response generalization was noted. Intermixing reinforced responses with nonreinforced responses resulted in the desired response generalization. Thus, one apparently viable strategy for programming setting generalization seems to be training in more than one structured environment. Moreover, intermixing trained and untrained stimulus events may facilitate response generalization. Garcia observed cross-setting response generalization only after an intermixing procedure had been instituted in two other settings. Other writers have programmed for generalization across settings without providing empirical demonstrations of effects to nontraining settings. Kazdin (1971), for example, in the application of a token economy system with retardates, developed an innovative strategy for effecting reinforcement across settings. Kazdin trained retardates to issue tokens to one another for experimenter-specified behavioral targets in several diverse settings within a sheltered workshop environment. As another example, Walker and Buckley (1972) compared three strategies for programming generalization of treatment gains across time and settings. The subjects of the study were 48 third to sixth graders who had been referred to an experimental school due to academic and social behavior problems. Following exposure to a token economy system that successfully modified their maladaptive behavior in the experimental classroom setting, the children were observed in their regular classroom situations. The three methods through which the experimenters attempted to achieve carryover of effect to the regular class setting were: (a) peer reprogramming, that is, structuring the setting so that classroom peers reinforced adaptive behavior on the part of the target subject; (b) equating stimulus conditions between the experimental and regular class settings (social and token reinforcement and academic materials), and (c) teacher training in behavior modification techniques. There was also a control group included with whom no attempt was made to program setting generalization. After the subjects had been returned to regular class settings for 2 months, the investigators found that the peer reprogramming group and the group wherein stimulus conditions had been equated exhibited significant carryover of experimental effects as compared to the control group. The control group and the teacher-training-in-behavior-modification group were not significantly different in their generalization-setting levels of appropriate behavior.

A third strategy that has been utilized to program for generalization has involved the rearrangement of salient stimuli in the training environment so as to approximate the setting events that exist in the natural environment. In practice, this generic strategy has included the rearrangement of events both antecedent and consequent to consumers' target behaviors. McLean and Raymore (1972) provided an example of this systematic rearrangement of antecedent stimulus conditions in articulation therapy as a means of programming generalized correct phoneme production. Their stimulus-shift articulation training program (McLean & Raymore, 1973) progresses subjects through a series of 12 successive changes in stimulus items designed to produce ultimately generalized conversational usage of the targeted phoneme. Another variety of antecedent stimuli item rearrangement is represented by studies that have employed several trainers in teaching the behavior so as to increase the likelihood that the target response will be exhibited in the presence of a large number of individuals (Corte, Wolf, & Locke, 1971; Lovaas & Simmons, 1969). Some investigators (Corte et al., 1971; Lovaas & Simmons, 1969) found that training by two or more agents was required to produce generalized effects to other adults in working to decelerate the self-injurious repertoires of behavior-disordered children. Similarly, in studies of the verbal greeting response of schizophrenic adults (Kale et al., 1968), the conversational speech form of retarded children (Garcia, 1974), and the gestural greeting of retarded children (Stokes, Baer, & Jackson, 1974), experimenters have reported that generalization became evident with nontraining experimenters only after training had been conducted by a number of experimenters. These result indicate that training across a few individuals is often sufficient to establish a consistent pattern of social responding in the presence of a large number of indiviuals.

Consequent events also have been systematically rearranged to program for generalization. One programming tactic in this regard has been to substitute natural for contrived reinforcers (Lent, 1968; Locke, 1969). Ferster (1972) has argued that any training program that seeks generalization must necessarily include provisions for eventually bringing consumers' targeted behavior under the control of reinforcers available in their natural environment. Many time, social-behavior modification programs have relied upon contrived reinforcing events without systematically substituting naturally available reinforcers (Kirby & Toler, 1970; Locke, 1969;

Whitman et al., 1970). Some researchers have held that behavior may be brought under the control of social reinforcement if such reinforcement is initially paired with the issuance of tokens or tangible reinforcers. The results of several investigations support this contention. Hopkins (1968) brought the smiling response of institutionalized retardates under social reinforcement control following a period of primary reinforcement. Kale et al. (1968) paired social reinforcement with cigarettes and subsequently faded the cigarettes in order to assume social control of the verbal greetings of schizophrenic adults. Reisinger (1972) substituted social reinforcement and ignoring for token reinforcement and token response cost tactics to maintain successfully therapeutic changes in the social responding of a female mental patient.

A related method by which to manipulate consequent events as an approach to programming generalization has involved altering the parameters of reinforcement existing in the training setting. For example, Schwartz and Hawkins (1970) demonstrated that setting generalization may be programmed through a delay of reinforcement tactic. Other investigators observed increases in subjects' performance in generalization settings subsequent to leaning schedules of reinforcement in the training environment (Kazdin & Polster, 1973; Meichenbaum, Bowers, & Ross, 1968). In actuality, setting generalization, when measured in a situation wherein trainer-controlled reinforcement, once administered, no longer occurs, constitutes exposing the subject to an extinction schedule. In principle, responding in situations wherein reinforcement was previously available, but no longer forthcoming, should be facilitated by exposing subjects to increasingly intermittent or leaned schedule of reinforcement (Ferster & Skinner, 1957). Kale et al. (1968) found generalized maintenance over a 3-month period in schizophrenic patients' greeting responses following intermittent reinforcement. Likewise, Kazdin and Polster (1973) found no decrease in the verbal interaction of a retarded adult in extinction sessions following intermittent token reinforcement. A second subject who was reinforced on a continuous basis, however, demonstrated an immediate decline in this social responding once the token reinforcers were withdrawn.

SUGGESTED RESEARCH

The primary issue in programming generalization from social-behavior interventions concerns methods of bringing the response of target subjects under the control of naturally occurring stimulus events. As Baer and Wolf (1970) have noted, generalization to other settings, over time, and to individuals other than trainers, cannot be expected unless the contingencies in the generalization setting support the newly acquired behavior. Recognizing this truism, Tharp and Wetzel (1969) have elaborated on the considerations involved in attempting to program a wide variety of behavioral targets in natural settings. They have presented a triadic model by which to effect therapeutic behavior changes within natural social systems. The essence of their plan rests on modifying problem behaviors within real-life contexts. They stress the logic of eliminating circumscribed training settings and involving persons indigenous to consumers' social systems as contingency managers. Their model represents a most direct technology for changing behavior in significant, natural social settings. Pertinent research regarding this technology should include cost–benefit analyses of behavior-change endeavors in artifically structured settings relative to behavior-modification programs conducted in natural settings. One recent investigation revealed maintenance of behavior changes and, in some cases, continued improvements over time (1 to 4 years following the termination of treatment) by autistic children, provided that their parents continued their behavior programs (Lovaas et al., 1973).

Another potentially fruitful avenue of investigation would seem to involve the refinement of observational systems so as to permit a more broad-scaled (yet behaviorally precise) perspective of the salient features of social systems wherein interventions are planned (Willems, 1974). Ecological recording systems provide a far more detailed picture of social behavior and its environmental context than is currently available through behavioral observation systems. For example, initial explication of specimen records could facilitate the determination of the most prevalent reinforcers and punishers available within counsumers' social systems as well as indicate the prevalent form of responding that is likely to result in either type of stimulus outcome. This information could make great contributions to designing behavioral interventions that maximize the probability that generalization will occur. Such information would permit change agents to better match environmental contexts and target subjects with available procedures.

The significance of easing target consumers' entries into natural communities of reinforcement is widely recognized. Little information is available, however, regarding the empirical selection of those target responses that are most likely to facilitate a subject's transition from contrived to naturally occurring communities of reinforcement. At present, no systematic guidelines exist concerning the responses that should be trained to maximize generalized effects. One general suggestion, however, seems warranted. It seems likely that the social behavior most often reinforced within a setting is that behavior which is most prevalent. Thus, it may be that withdrawn children should be taught to exhibit the social repertoires modal in their natural environment if generalized social reinforcement is desired. The typical vocal, social, gestural, and material-use responses emitted by the children in target subjects' natural settings might provide a useful index of target responses for social-behavior interventions. Along a similar vein, investigation is warranted regarding the identification and modification of behaviors that facilitate concurrent shifts in related behaviors. Cooke (1974), for example, found that the sharing behavior of many subjects in a generalization session increased, following a training period to teach smiling. The unit of behavior altered in any behavioral intervention may extend beyond the limits of the directly targeted response event(s). It may be that training in a few key social behaviors could bring about concurrent therapeutic change in a range of related responses.

Another primary area for research on programming generalization involves a consideration and analysis of the recipocal nature of social interaction. Reciprocity is now recognized to be an integral component of any equation involving interaction (Charlesworth & Hartup, 1967; Patterson & Reid, 1969; Strain et al., in press). Investigators have presented techniques for controlling reciprocal social-interaction patterns (Kazdin, 1971; Strain, Shores, & Abraham, in press; Strain & Timm, 1974; Straughan, Potter & Hamilton, 1965; Walker & Hops, 1973). As yet, however, there have been only limited demonstrations of generalized behavior change associated specifically with intervention strategies designed to induce changes in reciprocal-interaction patterns. This appears to be a promising area of future research. It may be that involving peers in reciprocal-response training with withdrawn children could be a key to facilitating generalization of the latter's trained responding. One technique that may alter generalization benefits is role playing to modify social performance. When target children are meeting social difficulty in several environmental settings, change agents may structure role-playing sessions to simulate the contingencies functioning across these problem settings. In this way, the change agents could attempt to teach the consumers the specific skills necessary for obtaining reinforcement in a variety of problem situations.

As a final suggestion, behavior-analytic investigators should begin to analyze the area of subject self-control as a method of achieving generalization (Kazdin, 1975). Research has shown that self-managed contingency arrangements are useful for accelerating children's behavior (Felixbrod & O'Leary, 1973; Glynn & Thomas, 1974; Lovitt & Curtiss, 1969). If subjects could be taught to self-reinforce their adaptive behaviors once they are under control through externally imposed contingencies, the implications for generalization would be enormous. Although little research is currently available regarding the effects of self-control techniques on stimulus and response generalization, some early findings (Meichenbaum & Goodman, 1971; Meichenbaum & Cameron, 1973) suggest positive outcomes. In fact, if children demonstrating atypical social repertoires could be successfully taught to maintain the constellation of behaviors necessary for adaptive functioning in their social network, difficulties associated with programming generalization would be attenuated greatly.

REFERENCES

Allen, K. E., Hart, B., Buell, J. S., Harris, F. R., & Wolf, M. M. Effects of social reinforcement on isolate behavior of a nursery school child. *Child Development,* 1964, *35,* 511–518.

Allen, K. E., Turner, K. D., & Everett, P. M. A behavior modification classroom for head start children with problem behaviors. *Exceptional Children,* 1970, *37,* 119–127.

Altman, K. Effects of cooperative response acquisition on social behavior during free-play. *Journal of Experimental Child Psychology,* 1971, *12,* 387–395.

Amidon, E. The isolate in children's groups: Changing his sociometric position. *Journal of Teacher Education,* 1961, *12,* 412–416.

Amidon, E., & Hoffman, C. Helping the socially isolated or rejected child. *National Elementary Principal,* 1963, *43,* 75–79.

Amidon, E. J., & Hoffman, C. Can teachers help the socially rejected? *Elementary School Journal,* 1965, *66,* 149–154.

Apolloni, T., & Cooke, T. P. Peer behavior conceptualized as a variable influencing infant and toddler development. *American Journal of Orthopsychiatry,* 1975, *45,* 4–17.

Ausubel, D. P. Theory and problems of child development. New York: Grune & Stratton, 1958.

Azrin, N. H., Holz, W., Ulrich, R., & Goldiamond, I. The control of the content of conversation through reinforcement. *Journal of the Experimental Analysis of Behavior*, 1961, *4*, 25–30.

Azrin, N. H., & Lindsley, O. R. The reinforcement of cooperation between children. *Journal of Abnormal and Social Psychology*, 1956, *52*, 100–102.

Baer, D. M., Peterson, R. F., & Sherman, J. A. The development of imitation by reinforcing behavioral similarity to a model. *Journal of the Experimental Analysis of Behavior*, 1967, *10*, 405–417.

Baer, D. M., & Sherman, J. A. Reinforcement control of generalized imitation in young children. *Journal of Experimental Child Psychology*, 1964, *1*, 37–49.

Baer, D. M., & Wolf, M. M. The entry into natural communities of reinforcement. In R. Ulrich, T. Stanhnick, & J. Mabry (Eds.), *Control of human behavior*. Glenview, Illinois: Scott, Foresman, 1970. Pp. 319–324.

Baer, D. M., Wolf, M. M., & Risley, T. R. Some current dimensions of applied behavior analysis. *Journal of Applied Behavior Analysis*, 1968, *1*, 91–97.

Baker, H. J., & Traphagen, V. *Diagnosis and treatment of behavior problem children*. New York: Macmillan, 1935.

Bandura, A. Social learning theory of identification process. In D. A. Goslin & D. C. Glass (Eds.), *Handbook of socialization theory and research*. New York: Rand McNally, 1966.

Bandura, A. *Principles of behavior modification*. New York: Holt, 1969.

Bandura, A., Grusec, J. E., & Menlove, F. L. Vicarious extinction of avoidance behavior. *Journal of Personality and Social Psychology*, 1967, *5*, 16–23.

Bandura, A., & Menlove, F. L. Factors determining vicarious extinction of avoidance behavior through symbolic modeling. *Journal of Personality and Social Psychology*, 1968, *8*, 99–108.

Bandura, A., & Walters, R. H. *Social learning and personality development*. New York: Holt, 1963.

Bijou, S. W. A functional analysis of retarded development. In N. R. Ellis (Ed.), *International review of research in mental retardation*. New York: Academic Press, 1966.

Bijou, S. W., Peterson, R. F., Harris, F. R., Allen, K. E., & Johnston, M. S. Methodology for experimental studies of young children in natural settings. *Psychological Record*, 1969, *19*, 177–210.

Birren, J. W. Psychological examinations of children who later became psychotic. *Journal of Abnormal and Social Psychology*, 1944, *39*, 84–96.

Blasdek, J. Behavior modification procedures applied to the isolate behavior of a nursery school child. *Educational Resources Information Center*, ED 041 635, 1968.

Bloom, B. S. *Stability and change in human characteristics*. New York: Wiley, 1964.

Blurton Jones, N. G. An ethological study of some aspects of social behavior of children in nursery school. In D. Morris (Ed.), *Primate ethology*. London: Weidenfeld Nicholson, 1967.

Bonney, M. E. Personality traits of socially unsuccessful children. *Jounral of Educational Psychology*, 1943, *34*, 449–473.

Bonney, M. E. Assessment of efforts to aid socially isolated elementary school pupils. *Journal of Educational Research*, 1971, *64*, 345–364.

Bower, E. M., Shellhamer, T. A., & Daily, J. M. School characteristics of male adolescents who later became schizophrenic. *American Journal of Orthopsychiatry*, 1960, *30*, 712–729.

Bowman, K. M. A study of the prepsychotic personality problem is certain psychoses. *American Journal of Orthopsychiatry*, 1934, *4*, 473–498.

Brackbill, Y. Extinction of the smiling response in infants as a function of reinforcement schedule. *Child Development*, 1958, *29*, 115–124.

Brigham, T. A., & Sherman, J. A. An experimental analysis of verbal imitation in preschool children. *Journal of Applied Behavior Analysis*, 1968, *1*, 151–158.

Buell, J., Stoddard, P., Harris, F. R., & Baer, D. M. Collateral social development accompanying reinforcement of outdoor play in a preschool child. *Journal of Applied Behavior Analysis*, 1968, *1*, 167–173.

Buswell, M. M. The relationship between the social structure of the classroom and the academic successes of the pupils. *Journal of Experimental Education*, 1953, *22*, 37–52.

Campbell, D. T., & Stanley, J. C. *Expermiental and quasiexperimental designs for research*. Chicago: Rand McNally, 1963.

Carpenter, F. *The Skinner primer: Behind freedom and dignity*. New York: Free Press, 1974.

Challman, R. C. Factors influencing friendship among preschool children. *Child Development*, 1932, *3*, 146–158.

Charlesworth, R., & Hartup, W. W. Positive social reinforcement in the nursery school peer group. *Child Development*, 1967, *38*, 993–1002.

Chennault, M. Improving the social acceptance of unpopular educable mentally retarded pupils in special classes. *American Journal of Mental Deficiency*, 1967, *72*, 455–458.

Clarzio, H. Stability of deviant behavior through time. *Mental Hygiene*, 1968, *52*, 288–293.

Clarzio, H. F., & McCoy, G. F. *Behavior disorders in preschool-aged children*. Scranton, Pennsylvania: Chandler, 1970.

Clement, P. N. Group play therapy and tangible reinforcers used to modify the behavior of 8 year old boys. *Educational Resources Information Center*, ED 016 997, 1967.

Cobb, J. A. The relationship of discrete classroom behaviors to fourth-grade academic achievement. *Oregon Research Institute Research Bulletin*, 1970, *10*, 1–10.

Cohen, D. J. Justin and his peers: An experimental analysis of a child's social world. *Child Development*, 1962, *33*, 697–717.

Cohen, D. J., & Lindsley, O. R. Catalysis of controlled leadership in cooperation by human stimulation. *Journal of Child Psychology and Psychiatry*, 1964, *5*, 119–137.

Cooke, T. P. Increasing levels of positive social–emotional behavior through the use of behavior analytic teaching tactics. Unpublished dissertation, George Peabody College, Nashville, Tennessee, 1974.

Cooke, T. P., Cooke, S. A., Wirtz, P. J., & Apolloni, T. Increasing a withdrawn child's level of social interaction through social reinforcement paired with a tonal stimulus. Unpublished manuscript, George Peabody College, Nash-ville,Tennessee, 1974.

Cooley, C. *Social organization*. New York: Scribners, 1909.

Corte, H. E., Wolf, M. M., & Locke, B. J. A comparison of procedures for eliminating self-injurious behavior of retarded adolescents. *Journal of Applied Behavior Analysis*, 1971, *4*, 201–213.

Cox, F. N. Sociometric status and individual adjustment before and after play therapy. *Journal of Abnormal and Social Psychology*, 1953, *48*, 354–356.

Dineen, M. A., & Garry, R. Effect of sociometric seating on a classroom cleavage. *Elementary School Journal*, 1956, *56*, 358–362.

Early, J. C. Attitude learning in children. *Journal of Educational Psychology*, 1968, *59*, 176–180.

Eysenck, H. J. The effect of psychotherapy: An evaluation. *Journal of Consulting Psychology*, 1952, *16*, 319–324.

Felixbrod, J. J., & O'Leary, K. D. Effects of reinforcement on children's academic behavior as a function of self-determined and externally imposed contingen-cies. *Journal of Applied Behavior Analysis*, 1973, *6*, 241–250.

Ferster, C. B. The repertoire of the autistic child in relation to principles of reinforcement. In L. Gottschalk (Ed.), *Methods of research in psychotherapy*. New York: Harper, 1965.

Ferster, C. B. Clinical reinforcement. *Seminar in Psychiatry*, 1972, *4*, 101–111.

Ferster, C. B., & Skinner, B. F. *Schedules of reinforcement*. New York: Appleton, 1957.

Flanders, N. A., & Havumaki, S. The effect of teacher–pupil contacts involving praise on the sociometric choices of students. *Journal of Educational Psychology*, 1960, *51*, 65–68.

Frazee, H. E. Children who later became schizophrenic. *Smith College Studies in Social Work*, 1953, *23*, 125–149.

Galvin, J. P., Quay, H. C., & Werry, J. S. Behavioral and academic gains of conduct problem children in different classroom settings. *Exceptional Children*, 1971, *37*, 441–446.

Garcia, E. The training and generalization of a conversational speech form in nonverbal retardates. *Journal of Applied Behavior Analysis*, 1974, *7*, 137–151.

Garcia, E. E., & DeHaven, E. J. Use of operant techniques in the establishment and generalization of language: A review and analysis. *American Journal of Mental Deficiency*, 1974, *79*, 169–178.

Gilbert, G. M. A survey of "referral problems" in metropolitan child guidance centers. *Journal of Clinical Psychology*, 1957, *13*, 37–42.

Gittelman, M. Behavior rehearsal as a technique in child treatment. *Journal of Child Psychology and Psychiatry*, 1965, *6*, 251–255.

Glynn, E. I., & Thomas, J. D. Effect of cueing on selfcontrol of classroom behavior. *Journal of Applied Behavior Analysis*, 1974, *7*, 199–306.

Gomber, J., & Mitchell, G. Preliminary report on adult male isolation-reared Rhesus monkeys caged with infants. *Developmental Psychology*, 1974, *10*, 298.

Green, E. H. Group play and quarrelling among preschool children. *Child Development*, 1933, *4*, 302–307.

Griffith, H., & Craighead, W. E. Generalization in operant speech therapy for misarticulation. *Journal of Speech and Hearing Research*, 1972, *37*, 485–494.

Hall, R. V., & Broden, M. Behavior changes in brain-injured children through social reinforcement. *Journal of Experimental Child Psychology,* 1967, *5,* 463–479.

Hanley, E. M. Review of research involving applied behavior in the classroom *Review of Educational Research,* 1970, *40,* 597–625.

Harlow, H. F., Gluck, J. P., & Suomi, S. J. Generalization of behavioral data between nonhuman and human animals. *American Psychologist,* 1972, *27,* 709–716.

Harlow, H. F., & Harlow, M. N. Social deprivation in monkeys. *Scientific American,* 1962, *207,* 136.

Harris, V. W., & Sherman, J. A. Effects of peer tutoring and consequences on the math performance of elementary classroom students. *Journal of Applied Behavior Analysis,* 1973, *6,* 587–597.

Hart, B. M., Reynolds, N. J., Baer, D. M., Brawley, E. R., & Harris, F. R. Effect of contingent and noncontingent social reinforcement on the cooperative play of a preschool child. *Journal of Applied Behavior Analysis,* 1968, *1,* 73–76.

Hartup, W. W. Peer interaction and social organization. In P. H. Mussen (Ed.), *Manual of child psychology.* (3rd ed.) New York: Wiley, 1970.

Hauserman, N., Walen, S. R., & Behling, M. Reinforced racial integration in the first grade: A study in generalization. *Journal of Applied Behavior Analysis,* 1973, *6,* 193–200.

Havelkova, M. Follow-up study of seventy-one children diagnosed as psychotic in pre-school age. *American Journal of Orthopsychiatry,* 1968, *38,* 846–857.

Heinstein, M. *Behavior problems of young children in California.* Berkeley, California: Bureau of Maternal and Child Health, 1969.

Hewett, F. M. Teaching speech to an autistic child through operant conditioning. *American Journal of Orthopsychiatry,* 1965, *35,* 927–936.

Hingtgen, J. N., Sanders, B. M., & Deyer, M. K. Shaping cooperative responses in early childhood schizophrenics. In L. Ullman & L. Krasner (Eds.), *Case studies in behavior modification.* New York: Holt, 1965. Pp. 130–138.

Hingtgen, J. N., & Trost, F. C. Shaping cooperative responses in early childhood schizophrenics. II. Reinforcement of mutual physical contact and vocal responses. In R. Ulrich, T. Stachnick, & J. Mabry (Eds.), *Control of human behavior.* Glenview, Illinois: Scott, Foresman, 1966. Pp. 110–113.

Holmes, F. B. An experimental investigation of a method of overcoming children's fears. *Child Development,* 1936, *7,* 6–30.

Hopkins, B. L. Effects of candy and social reinforcement, instructions, and reinforcement schedule learning on the modification and maintenance of smiling. *Journal of Applied Behavior Analysis,* 1968, *1,* 121–129.

Jackson, T. A., Stanex, E., Lane, E., & Dominguez, K. Studies in the trasposition of learning by children. I. Relative vs. absolute responses as a function of amount of training. *Journal of Experimental Psychology,* 1938, *23,* 573–600.

Johnson, M. W. The effect on behavior of variation in amount of play equipment. *Child Development,* 1935, *6,* 56–68.

Johnston, M. K., Kelley, C. S., Harris, F. R., & Wolf, M. M. An application of reinforcement principles to development of motor skills of a young child. *Child Development,* 1966, *37,* 379–387.

Kale, R. J., Kaye, P. A., Whelan, P. A., & Hopkins, B. L. The effects of reinforcement on the modification, maintenance, and generalization of social responses of mental patients. *Journal of Applied Behavior Analysis,* 1968, *1,* 307–314..

146   Strain, Cooke, and Apolloni

Kasanin, J., & Veo, L. A study of the school adjustments of children who later in life became psychotic. *American Journal of Orthopsychiatry*, 1932, 2, 212–227.
Kazdin, A. E. Toward a client administered token reinforcement program. *Education and Training of the Mentally Retarded*, 1971, 6, 52–55.
Kazdin, A. E. *Behavior modification in applied settings.* Homewood, Illinois: Dorsey Press, 1975.
Kazdin, A. E., & Craighead, W. E. Behavior modification in special education. In L. Mann & D. A. Sabatino (Eds.), *The first review of special education.* Philadelphia: Buttonwood Farms, 1973.
Kazdin, A. E., & Polster, R. Intermittent token reinforcement and response maintenance in extinction. *Behavior Therapy*, 1973, 4, 386–391.
Kerstetler, L. M., & Sargent, J. Reassignment therapy in the classroom. *Sociometry*, 1940, 3, 292–306.
Kinney, E. E. A study of peer-group social acceptability of the fifth grade level in a public school. *Journal of Educational Research*, 1953, 47, 57–64.
Kirby, F. D., & Toler, H. C. Modification of preschool isolate behavior: A case study. *Journal of Applied Behavior Analysis*, 1970, 3, 309–314.
Kranzler, G. D., Mayer, G. R., Dyer, C. O., & Munger, P. F. Counseling with elementary school children: An experimental study. *Personnel and Guidance Journal*, 1966, 44, 944–949.
Lazarus, A. A. The elimination of children's phobias by deconditioning. In H. J. Eysenck (Ed.), *Behavior therapy and the neuroses.* New York: Pergamon Press, 1960.
Lent, J. R. Mimosa Cottage: Experiment in hope. *Psychology Today*, 1968, 2, 50–58.
Levin, G., & Simmons, J. Response to food and praise by emotionally disturbed boys. *Psychological Reports*, 1962, 11, 539–546. (a)
Levin, G., & Simmons, J. Response to praise by emotionally disturbed boys. *Psychological Reports*, 1962, 11, 10. (b)
Levison, C. A. Use of the peer group in the socialization of the isolate child. *Educational Resources Information Center*, ERI ED 054 858, 1971.
Levitt, E. E. The results of psychotherapy with children: An evaluation. *Journal of Consulting Psychology*, 1957, 21, 189–196.
Lindsley, O. R. Experimental analysis of cooperation and competition. In T. Verhave (Ed.), *The experimental analysis of behavior: Selected readings.* New York: Appleton, 1966.
Lipe, D., & Jung, S. M. Manipulating incentives to enhance school learning. *Review of Educational Research*, 1971, 41, 249–280.
Locke, B. Verbal conditioning with retarded subjects: Establishment or reinstatement of effective reinforcing consequences. *American Journal of Mental Deficiency*, 1969, 73, 621–626.
Lovaas, O. I., Berberich, J. P., Perloff, B. F., & Schaeffer, B. Acquisition of imitative speech in schizophrenic children. *Science*, 1966, 151, 705–707.
Lovaas, O. I., Freitag, G., Kinder, M. I., Rubenstein, B. D., Schaeffer, B., & Simmons, J. Q. Experimental studies in childhood schizophrenia. II. Establishment of social reinforcers. Paper presented to Western Psychological Association, 1964.
Lovaas, O. I., Freitag, L., Nelson, K., & Whalen, C. The establishment of imitation

and its use for the development of complex behavior in schizophrenic children. *Behavior Research and Therapy*, 1967, *5*, 171–181.

Lovaas, O. I., Koegel, R., Simmons, J. Q., & Long, J. S. Some generalization and follow-up measures on autistic children in behavior therapy. *Journal of Applied Behavior Analysis*, 1973, *6*, 131–166.

Lovaas, O. I., & Simmons, J. Q. Manipulation of self-destruction in three retarded children. *Journal of Applied Behavior Analysis*, 1969, *2*, 143–157.

Lovitt, T. C., & Curtiss, K. A. Academic response rate as a function of teacher- and self-imposed contingencies. *Journal of Applied Behavior Analysis*, 1969, *2*, 49–53.

Lyon, V. L. Conditioning and generalization of a verbal response in hospitalized schizophrenics. Unpublished doctoral dissertation, Univ. of Kansas, 1971.

Marshall, H. R., & McCandless, B. R. A study in prediction of social behavior of preschool children. *Child Development*, 1957, *28*, 149–159.

Mayer, G. R., Kransler, G. D., & Matthews, W. A. Elementary school counseling and peer relations. *Personnel and Guidance Journal*, 1967, *46*, 360–365.

McCandless, B. R., & Hoyt, J. M. Sex, ethnicity, and play preferences of preschool children. *Journal of Abnormal and Social Psychology*, 1961, *62*, 683–685.

McLean, J. E., & Raymore, S. *Programmatic research on a systematic articulation therapy program: Carry-over of phoneme responses to untrained situations for normal-learning public school children.* Parsons Research Center, Report No. 6, Kansas Center for Research in Mental Retardation and Human Development, July, 1972.

McLean, J., & Raymore, S. *Project MORE: Stimulus shift articulation program.* (Experimental Edition) Bureau of Child Research, Univ. of Kansas, 1973.

Meichenbaum, D. H., Bowers, K., & Ross, R. R. Modification of classroom behavior of institutionalized female adolescent offenders. *Behavior Research and Therapy*, 1968, *6*, 343–353.

Meichenbaum, D. H., & Cameron, E. Training schizophrenics to talk to themselves: A means of developing attentional controls. *Behavior Therapy*, 1973, *4*, 515–534.

Meichenbaum, D. H., & Goodman, J. Training impulsive children to talk to themselves: A means for developing self-control. *Journal of Abnormal Psychology*, 1971, *77*, 115–126.

Michael, C. M., Morris, D. P., & Soroker, E. Follow-up studies of shy, withdrawn children. II. Relative incidence of schizophrenia. *American Journal of Orthopsychiatry*, 1957, *27*, 331–337.

Miller, N. E., & Dollard, J. *Social learning and imitation.* New Haven: Yale Univ. Press, 1941.

Moreno, J. L. Who shall survive? *Nervous and Mental Disease Monograph No. 58.* Washington, D.C., 1934.

Moreno, J. L. *Psychodrama.* Vol. I. New York: Beacon House, 1946.

Moreno, S. L., & Jennings, H. H. Sociometric methods of grouping and regrouping, with reference to authoritative and democratic methods of grouping. *Sociometry*, 1944, *7*, 397–414.

Moreno, Z. T. Psychodramatic rules, techniques, and adjunctive methods. *Group Psychotherapy*, 1965, *18*, 73–86.

Morris, D. P., Soroker, E., & Burrus, G. Follow-up studies of shy, withdrawn children. I. Evaluation of later adjustment. *American Journal of Orthopsychiatry,* 1954, *24,* 743–754.

Mowrer, D. E. Transfer of training in articulation therapy. *Journal of Speech and Hearing Disorders,* 1971, *36,* 427–446.

Newbouig, M. H., & Klausmeier, H. J. *Teaching in the elementary school.* New York: Harper, 1969.

Northway, M. L. Outsiders: A study of the personality patterns of children least acceptable to their age mates. *Sociometry,* 1944, *7,* 10–25.

O'Connor, R. D. Modification of social withdrawal through symbolic modeling. *Journal of Applied Behavior Analysis,* 1969, *1,* 15–22.

O'Connor, R. D. Relative efficacy of modeling, shaping, and the combined procedures for modification of social withdrawal. *Journal of Abnormal Psychology,* 1972, *79,* 327–334.

O'Leary, K. D., & Drabman, R. Token reinforcement programs in the classroom: A Review. *Psychological Bulletin,* 1971, *75,* 379–398.

O'Neal, P., & Robins, L. N. Childhood patterns predictive of adult schizophrenia: A follow-up study. *American Journal of Psychiatry,* 1958, *115,* 385–391.

Osgood, C. E. The similarity paradox in human learning: A resolution. *Psychological Review,* 1949, *56,* 132–143.

Paloutzian, R. F., Hasazi, J., Streifel, J., & Edgar, C. L. Promotion of positive social interaction in severely retarded children. *American Journal of Mental Deficiency,* 1971, *75,* 519–524.

Parten, M. B. Social play among preschool children. *Journal of Abnormal and Social Psychology,* 1933, *28,* 136–147.

Patterson, G. R., & Reid, J. Reciprocity and coercion: Two facets of social systems. In C. Neuringer & J. Michael (Eds.), *Behavior modification in clinical psychology.* New York: Appleton, 1969.

Piaget, J., & Inhelder, B. *The psychology of the child.* New York: Basic Books, 1969.

Quay, H. C. Dimensions of problem behavior and educational programming. In P. S. Giaubord (Ed.), *Children against schools.* Chicago: Follett, 1969.

Quilitch, H. R., & Risley, T. R. The effects of play materials on social play. *Journal of Applied Behavior Analysis,* 1973, *6,* 573–578.

Rardin, D. R., & Moan, C. E. Peer interaction and cognitive development. *Child Development,* 1971, *42,* 1685–99.

Reese, H. W., & Lipsitt, L. P. *Experimental child psychology.* New York: Academic Press, 1970.

Reisinger, J. J. The treatment of "anxiety-depression" via positive reinforcement and response cost. *Journal of Applied Behavior Analysis,* 1972, *5,* 125–130.

Reppucci, N. D., & Saunders, J. T. Social psychology of behavior modification: Problems of implementation in natural settings. *American Psychologist,* 1974, *29,* 649–660.

Reynolds, G. S. *A primer of operant conditioning.* New York: Scott, Foresman, 1967.

Rhodes, W. C. Psychological techniques and theory applied to behavior modification. *Exceptional Children,* 1962, *28,* 333–338.

Robins, L. N. *Deviant children grown up: A sociological and psychiatric study of sociopathic personality.* Baltimore: Williams & Wilkins, 1966.

Robins, L. N., & O'Neal, P. Mortality, mobility and crime: Problem children thirty years later. *American Sociological Review,* 1958, *23,* 162–171.

Rogers, M. E., Lilenfield, A. M., & Pasamanick, B. *Prenatal and paranatal factors in the development of childhood behavior disorders.* Baltimore: Johns Hopkins Univ. Press, 1955.

Sailor, W. Reinforcement and generalization of productive plural allomorphs in two retarded children. *Journal of Applied Behavior Analysis,* 1971, *4,* 305–310.

Schwartz, M. L., & Hawkins, R. P. Application of delayed reinforcement procedures to the behavior of an elementary school child. *Journal of Applied Behavior Analysis,* 1970, *3,* 85–96.

Sheppard, W. C. Operant control of infant vocal and motor behavior. *Journal of Experimental Child Psychology,* 1959, *7,* 36–51.

Sibley, S. A., Abbott, M. S., Stark, P. A., Bullock, S. J., & Leonhardt, T. M. Modification by social reinforcement of deficient social behavior of disadvantaged kindergarten children. *Educational Resources Information Center,* ED 043 381, 1967.

Sidman, M. *Tactics of scientific research. Evaluating the experimental data in psychology.* New York: Basic Books, 1960.

Singer, H. Certain aspects of personality and their relation to certain group modes, and constancy of friendship choices. *Journal of Educational Research,* 1951, *45,* 33–42.

Skinner, B. F. *The behavior of organisms: An experimental analysis.* New York: Appleton, 1938.

Skinner, B. F. *Science and human behavior.* New York: Macmillan, 1953.

Skinner, B. F. Two synthetic social relations. *Journal of the Experimental Analysis of Behavior,* 1962, *5,* 531–533.

Skinner, B. F. *About behaviorism.* New York: Knopf, 1974.

Sommer, R., & Ross, H. Social interaction on a geriatric ward. *International Journal of Social Psychology,* 1958, *4,* 128–133.

Sorokin, P. A., & Grove, D. S. Notes on the friendly and antagonistic behavior of nursery school children. In P. A. Sorokin (Ed.), *Explorations in altruistic love and behavior.* Boston: Beacon Press, 1950.

Stendler, C. B., Damrin, D., & Haines, A. C. Studies in cooperation and competition. I: The effects of working for group and individual rewards on the social climate of children's groups. *Journal of Genetic Psychology,* 1951, *79,* 173–198.

Stokes, T. F., Baer, D. M., & Jackson, R. L. Programming the generalization of a greeting response in four retarded children. *Journal of Applied Behavior Analysis,* 1974, *7,* 599–610.

Strain, P. S., Shores, R. E., & Abraham, M. M. The development and control of reciprocal social interaction between behaviorally handicapped preschool children. *Journal of Applied Behavior Analysis,* in press.

Strain, P. S., & Timm, M. A. An experimental analysis of social interaction between a behaviorally disordered child and her classroom peers. *Journal of Applied Behavior Analysis,* 1974, *1,* 583–590.

Straughan, J. H., Potter, W. K., & Hamilton, S. H. The behavioral treatment of an elective mute. *Journal of Child Psychology and Psychiatry,* 1965, *6,* 125–130.

Suomi, S. J., & Harlow, H. F. Social rehabilitation of isolate-reared monkeys. *Developmental Psychology,* 1972, *6,* 487–496.

Terrace, H. S. Stimulus control. In W. K. Honiz (Ed.), *Operant behavior: Areas of research and application.* New York: Appleton, 1966.

Tharp, R. G., & Wetzel, R. J. *Behavior modification in the natural environment*. New York: Academic Press, 1969.

Thorndike, E. L. *Selected writings from a connectionist's psychology*. New York: Appleton, 1949.

Van Alstnyne, D., & Hattwick, L. A. A follow-up study of the behavior of nursery school children. *Child Development*, 1939, *19*, 43–72.

Wahler, R. G. Child–child interactions in free field settings: Some experimental analyses. *Journal of Experimental Child Psychology*, 1967, *5*, 278–293.

Walker, H. M., & Buckley, N. K. Programming generalization and maintenance of treatment effects across time and settings. *Journal of Applied Behavior Analysis*, 1972, *5*, 209–224.

Walker, H. M., & Hops, H. The use of group and individual reinforcement contingencies in the modification of social withdrawal. In L. A. Hamerlynch, L. C. Handy, & E. J. Mash (Eds.), *Behavior change: Methodology, concepts, and practice*. Champaign, Illinois: Research Press, 1973. Pp. 269–307.

Whitman, T. L., Mercurio, J. R., & Caponigri, V. Development of social responses in two severely retarded children. *Journal of Applied Behavior Analysis*, 1970, *3*, 133–138.

Willems, E. P. Behavioral technology and behavioral ecology. *Journal of Applied Behavior Analysis*, 1974, *7*, 151–165.

Subject Index

WITHDRAWN